pornography
the secret history of civilization

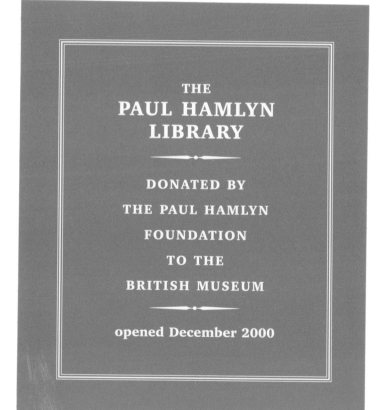

pornography

the secret history of civilization

ISABEL TANG

Introduction by Fenton Bailey

First published 1999 by Channel 4 Books,
an imprint of Macmillan Publishers Ltd,
25 Eccleston Place, London, SWlW 9NF,
Basingstoke and Oxford
Associated companies throughout the world
www.macmillan.co.uk

ISBN 0 7522 1792 5

1 3 5 7 9 8 6 4 2

A CIP catalogue record for this book is available from
the British Library.

Inside design by Dan Newman/Perfect Bound Design
Colour reproduction by Speedscan, Basildon, Essex
Printed and bound in Great Britain by Butler and Tanner, Frome, Somerset

While every effort has been made to trace copyright holders for illustrations featured in this book,
the publishers will be glad to make proper acknowledgements in future editions in the event
that any regrettable omissions have occurred at the time of going to press.

This book accompanies the television series
'Pornography: The Secret History of Civilization' made by World of Wonder for Channel 4.
Series producers: Fenton Bailey and Randy Barbato

Acknowledgements

First, I should like to acknowledge my debt to all those academics who have made the history of pornography such a new and dynamic field, and in particular I should like to thank the interviewees and scholars quoted in this book. I am also grateful to the following people: Fenton Bailey for getting the whole project off the ground, against the odds; World of Wonder, particularly Sarah Mortimer and Sam Bickley for helping even when they were buried themselves; Kate French for working so hard on finding the pictures; Julian, whose Herculean efforts and skateboard mercy dashes across London will not be forgotten; David Buxton who heroically battled with my technology; Rose Foot who amazed me with her skilful excavations; Lesley Levene, whose rigour kept me on the straight and narrow; Amy for her much appreciated contribution to Chapter Seven; Katy Carrington, my editor, whose great patience, good humour and commitment made this book happen; Kate Middleton whose friendship and support made it possible for me to take it on in the first place; Marian and Cecil for somehow always being on the end of the phone when I needed them; and most of all Tim, who kept me sane.

ISABEL TANG

Producing a book of a television series totally depends on the contributions and co-operation of the production team, all of whom worked heroically to deliver the series while the book was being put together. The directors of the series, Kate Williams ('The Road To Ruin' and 'Pornotopia'), Chris Rodley ('The Sacred and Profane' and 'Twentieth Century Foxy') and Dev Varma ('The Mechanical Eye'), all did a superlative job. They were assisted by associate producers Sarah Mortimer and Sam Bickley and assistant producers Matilda Mitchell and Anna Gien, who left no stone unturned in telling the story of 'Pornography'. The schedule demanded having three camera crews shooting simultaneously all over the world for three months, a feat coolly masterminded by production manager Helena Bullivant, and smoothly brought off by production co-ordinator Elaine Goodwin and production secretary Claire Bugden. Almost as daunting a task was gathering and clearing all the pictures for the book, brilliantly managed by Kate French, with Jo Chiles who was also the series film researcher. Thanks also to everyone at World of Wonder, both in the Los Angeles and London offices, particularly Neil Beasley, Annette Gordon, Michelle Kinsler, Guy Woodall, Julian Wallinger, Harry Knapp, Scott Franse, Ed Magana, Tiffany Flynn and Thairin Smothers; and above all to my partner and series co-producer Randy Barbato who remained calm in the face of adversity. Thanks also to my agent Cat Ledger and to Miles Chapman; to Channel 4 Books, and last, but not least, a very special thanks to editor Katy Carrington who pulled it all together.

FENTON BAILEY, C4 series executive producer.

For my mother and father who will bear this dedication
with good humour, for which I am grateful.

Contents

Introduction

[*by Fenton Bailey*]

When I tell people that I have been working on six one-hour documentaries recounting, for the first time, the history of pornography, they take this in a number of different ways. One or two are genuinely interested, but few can resist making some kind of judgement, expressing varying degrees of distaste, from outright disapproval to a liberal yawn. At the same time almost everyone is too polite not to feign interest and for this they pay dearly as they are pinned against the wall and harangued about the finer points of pornographic history until they make a determined attempt to escape.

My interest in pornography dates back to when I was a student and co-editor of *Isis*, the Oxford University magazine. Determined to make a splash in the new year of 1981, we decided to review the state of the porn business in Britain. When our 'Empire of the Senses' issue hit the stands, WHSmith withdrew it from their shelves. When I innocently told the *Daily Telegraph* that I thought newsagents who stocked girlie magazines were being hypocritical, WHSmith's lawyers made threatening noises. Then the University Faculty got involved. Then the police. It was fun for about five minutes. Finally, all the fuss died down. Years later the person who had co-authored the *Isis* article read me a letter his mother had written to him, cautioning him to avoid me since I was someone who apparently enjoyed masturbating in public. Although we laughed it off at the time, the gibe has come to encapsulate how something that started out as a bit of a lark turned ugly. The common intensity of the various reactions gave me a glimpse of what might happen to those who dared to broach the societal taboo surrounding pornography.

Since then the hysteria pornography tends to provoke has dwindled. Somewhat. I overestimated the sea change when in 1988 *Porn Gold* by David Hebditch and Nick Anning was published.[1] This was the first book to look at the adult entertainment business without a moral axe to grind, as is evident from its initial observation that the adult business as a whole is a global concern generating billions of dollars to enhance the bottom line of such blue-chip corporations as Sony and Kodak, and institutions as august as the Vatican. The book also detailed the operations of Europe's porn barons, painting, contrary to expectation, an atmosphere of corporate professionalism. Inspired by their book to try and make a history of pornography for television, I got the authors on the phone. Good luck, they said. Dispirited by the way the book had been

◁ Sylvia Kristel in *Emmanuelle*, 1974. A classic early soft-core film that nudged pornography closer to the mainstream.

▷ Woody Harrelson and Courtney Love in the *People Versus Larry Flynt*. The contemporary porno milieu: pornographer Larry Flynt was lionized in this Hollywood bio-pic.

generally ignored by reviewers, they were in no doubt that a television history of porn would never fly.

The first proposal went off to Channel 4 in 1989. It was flat-out rejected, as were many subsequent approaches. In 1992 I pitched the idea to the BBC. They liked it, beginning a tortuous three-year process of development that would end in failure. During this time I had lunch with Peter Webb, who had written the then definitive academic text about pornography called *The Erotic Arts*, published in 1975.[2]

Like the authors of *Porn Gold*, he too seemed less than buoyant about the experience of having his book published. Teaching his course on the same subject at Middlesex University had rendered him a pariah among other academics and he had even received death threats, about which the police were not remotely sympathetic. Indeed, as far as the police and other guardians of the so-called public good were concerned, Peter Webb was the enemy. Nevertheless, he was politely encouraging while also downplaying any notion that such a series would ever be commissioned by a major broadcaster. I felt I had proved Peter Webb wrong as through 1994 the BBC edged closer to commissioning the series. It looked like we were on our way, but we weren't. A few weeks later a newspaper article appeared framing the project as an outrageous use of licence-payers' money. It was accompanied by a dismissal by the BBC: they had no plans to pursue such a project. And that was the end of that.

After six years of trying, I was ready to call it a day. However, marching in step with these failed efforts, pornography was edging its way from the margins into the mainstream. The movement began in universities, where academics were studying pornography's rich heritage. In 1987 Walter Kendrick published his seminal text *The Secret Museum*.[3] In 1989 Linda Williams published *Hard Core: Power, Pleasure and the*

'*Frenzy of the Visible*'[4], in 1991 Bernard Arcand published *The Jaguar and the Anteater*[5], and in 1993 Lynn Hunt edited a collection of essays that was published under the collective title *The Invention of Pornography*.[6] At the same time, porn studies were beginning to be taught on American campuses. In 1993 Constance Penley started teaching a course on pornographic film at the University of California at Santa Barbara. The following year Linda Williams began teaching her course 'Pornographies On/Scene' at Berkeley. She argued that pornography was becoming more high profile, with the example of Senator Jesse Helms making an exhibition of himself by waving Robert Mapplethorpe pictures on the floor of the House in protest at the National Endowment for the Arts funding such controversial work.

Old school disapproval of such activity still lingers. Recently *The New Yorker* ran an article acknowledging this scholarly trend.[7] While applauding the pornologists for 'criticizing the premises of cultural authority', the article pulled back from the brink of endorsement by questioning in its final sentence if we really needed a curriculum dedicated to porn: 'After all a blue movie is still a blue movie.' Once again the liberal yawn, distaste disguised as boredom and the hint that such things do not merit genuine study.

△ A hard-core spoof of the Monica Lewinsky scandal.

Running parallel with this academic interest, pornography was even becoming chic in pop culture. Today there is a sports leisure clothing line called Porn Star, which trades on blazing Porn Star across T-shirts and baseball caps. Calvin Klein appropriated the standard trademarks of mid-1970s porn flicks – such as wood veneer and shag-pile carpeting – for his provocative ad campaigns, and music videos also adopted the look, most memorably Fiona Apple's *Criminal*. In addition to the shag and veneer, the video laid on thick those 1970s hues of olive greens, dark purples and chocolate browns. Rarely has the ugly ever looked so beautiful. Directed by Mark Romanek the clip won an MTV Music Video Award in 1997. Hollywood has even joined in, sanitizing the business of sleaze first in 1996 with *The People Versus Larry Flynt*, a lionizing biopic of the founder of *Hustler* magazine and then with Burt Reynolds playing a lovable pornapreneur in *Boogie Nights* in 1997.

But perhaps there is no greater signifier of today's porno milieu than the Monica Lewinsky scandal, which played out on the world stage like a talk-show episode. The *New York Times* decided that 'blow job' was fit to print, *Penthouse* published a portrait of

△ (Top) *Boogie Nights,* starring Burt Reynolds and Mark Wahlberg, proved that pornography could be box-office gold. (Bottom) Heather Graham and Mark Wahlberg in another scene from the film.

Bill Clinton collaged out of thousands of hard-core stills and an enterprising company released *Scenes from the Oral Office*, a hard-core parody of the Starr Report.

One other change that did not generate international headlines but was hugely significant for our projected television series was that Janey Walker, who had championed the idea at the BBC, had moved to Channel 4, followed a few months later by BBC chief Michael Jackson, who had also been behind it.

Resurrected, the question now was – were we too late?

While pornography is still illegal in Britain, the media had circumvented the ban by creating quasi-porn. Newsagents' shelves were bursting with magazines showing sex on their covers. *Sky, Loaded* and *FHM* have all found circulation gold with cheery smut, while the *Erotic Review* has enjoyed similar success by ploughing a higher brow. Meanwhile, television has *Eurotrash* and *Sex and Shopping*, a shockumentary series ostensibly debating censorship in the context of as much shagging as possible.

This riot of pseudo-porn, however, conspicuously dances around the margins of pornography itself, and even though more and more toes are testing the moral waters, what is generally understood and accepted as hard-core pornography still remains a forbidden zone – at least in the UK. In this environment it seemed that the straightforward history of pornography, as distinct from the moral brouhaha forever swirling around it, was a story yet to be told. It also seemed that by strictly limiting ourselves to the history we might, in contrast to the years of debate from the all too familiar angles of Christianity, feminism and censorship, succeed in shedding some light where others had barely even managed to generate heat.

But the clarity of this approach almost immediately became bogged down as we agonized over the title. Would this be a history of porn or erotica (*The History of Erotica* had been suggested as a working title). The popular wisdom is that if something is erotic it can be sexual, even explicitly so, and that is OK, in contrast to something that is pornographic, which is not OK. As art critic Edward Lucie-Smith points out, parents have no problem looking at Bronzino's *Venus, Cupid, Folly and Time*, which depicts a naked woman being French-kissed by a naked boy who is not only under-age but also her son, while they are having kittens about their kids seeing things on the Internet. The difference, then, is not in the content but the context. All too often the 'erotic' is a coyism, a veil used to aesthetically redeem the unacceptably raw expression of sex.

For the wretched and phoney distinction between the erotic and pornographic we have D. H. Lawrence to thank. Bill Thompson of Reading University has perhaps put it most succinctly: 'Lawrence claimed he could detect a difference between pornography and his art where there is none.' Strangely sanctified in the popular imagination as the Priest of Love, Lawrence really was little different from a fire and brimstone preacher who used super-heated metaphors to berate his audience into submission. To conjure up his particular brand of Hell, he relied on the same old preacher's lexicon, augmenting it with imagery concerning the industrial and all things modern (for example, he even saw Cubism as a form of mechanized pornography). Of all his sermonizing novels, *Lady Chatterley's Lover* was perhaps the most shrill. He demonized the mechanical, railed against the anal, condemned the masturbatory and stirred them altogether in the furnace of his prose to create the pornographic, which he took every opportunity to denounce as the cancer of the modern age, gnawing away at the sanctity of love. He then took his frenzied concoction and poured it into the mould of Sir Clifford Chatterley, a crippled war hero portrayed by Lawrence as a masturbatory emasculate. Part man, part machine, and wholly repugnant, Clifford comes over as a modern Dr Frankenstein, maniacally and fetishistically obsessed with machines, intent on raping the landscape and destroying all the natural beauty around him. All in contrast of course to Lady Chatterley herself, whose sexuality is seen as all things bright and beautiful.

Lawrence's novel is organized around this dichotomy between natural lovemaking (the erotic) and mechanical masturbation (the pornographic). It mirrors a traditional way of separating the wheat of the erotic art from the chaff of pornographic rubbish that is centuries old. In 1668 Samuel Pepys picked up a copy of an early erotic novel, *L'Ecole des Filles*. Having read it and pleasured himself, he threw the 'idle roguish book' on the fire. In short, if you jerk off to it, it can have no other redeeming value. Three centuries later, we may be more liberal when it comes to actually burning books, but the same crude arousal test persists, reinforced by the high-profile trial of *Lady Chatterley's Lover* as a test case of the Obscene Publications Act of 1959 when it was eventually published in the UK, some thirty years after Lawrence wrote it. In the trial the defence took their cue from Lawrence's hysterical philosophy of the pornographic as some sort of masturbatory grotesque and lined up a parade of scholars and authors to bear witness to this, blinding the prosecution with their erudition and arguing that Lawrence's work, far from being obscene and pornographic, was the opposite – erotic, artistic literature. It was a brilliant legal scam, a perfect counter to the absurd wording of the Obscene Publications Act, to which we owe the popular definition of pornography: 'that which has a tendency to deprave and corrupt'. Those words have taken on the force of an eleventh commandment. Canonizing *Lady Chatterley's Lover* as a work of art not only reinforced the notion of the pornographic as something likely to deprave and corrupt, it also suggested that the erotic was something finer minds could enjoy without risk.

Once we had decided that the series would be a history of pornography rather than erotica, how would we define it? What were the earliest definitions of pornography? One such appears in *Webster's Dictionary* in 1864: 'licentious painting or literature, especially the painting anciently employed to decorate walls of rooms devoted to bacchanalian orgies', referring back to the shocking discoveries at Pompeii in the eighteenth century. In *The Secret Museum*, Walter Kendrick explores the shock that confronted the early

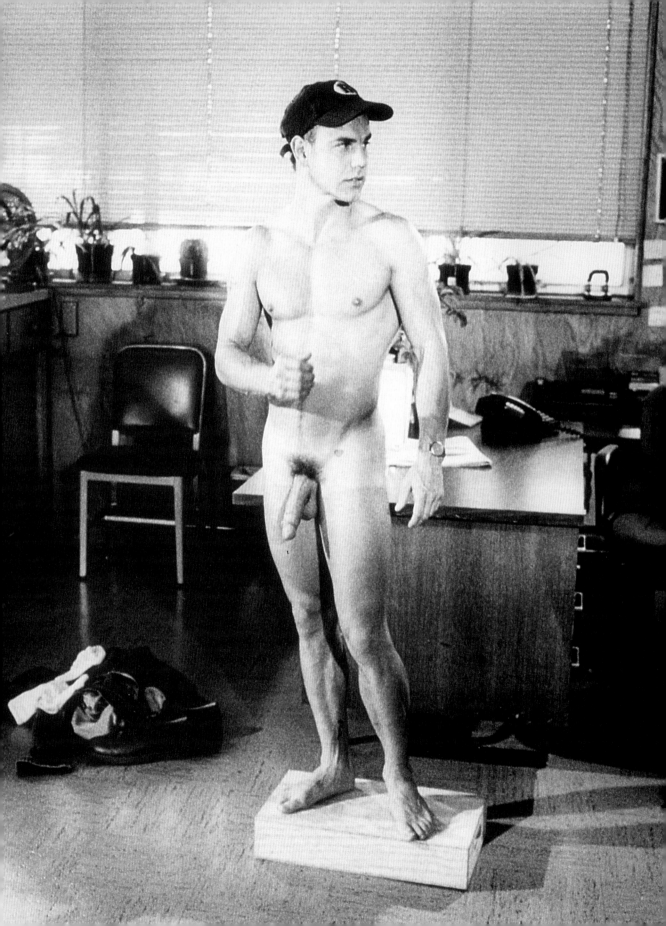

Victorians when they first learned of the finds from Pompeii. The question that faced them was what to do with the abundance of lewd artefacts they found that were obviously part of everyday life for the ancient Romans? Such objects had no place in polite society, and yet they could not possibly be thrown away. The solution was to place them in a 'secret museum', where 'gentlemen with appropriate demeanour (and ready cash for the custodian), would be admitted to the locked chamber where controversial items lurked; women, children and the poor of both sexes and all ages were excluded.'[9] The idea of the secret museum caught on with museums all over Europe setting up their own restricted collections, from the l'Enfer in Paris to the Private Case at the British Library in London.

Reading *The Secret Museum* was both enlightening and frustrating. Enlightening because I realized that if pornography is a social construct, and a relatively recent one at that, the attempt to define it is a Gordian knot, a trick question, since essentially no such thing exists. It is only naming the thing that creates it; it is an interpretative category. So much of the material labelled as pornography needs no such classification: to label it as such is little more than a wilful rhetorical act that has no other meaning. Instead of being a concretely, separately defined entity, much so-called pornography belongs as a part of the history of civilization, merely representing the development of sexual representation, and is quite undeserving of any secret shame.

In telling the history of pornography the purpose of our series was suddenly clear: to deconstruct the secret museum, to declassify the secret history of civilization. But this was where the frustration kicked in, because such a project was also doomed to failure. One of the most abundant subjects of images and artefacts found among the ruins of Pompeii, and indeed in ancient sites generally, was that of the erect phallus. Today, in spite of our apparently liberal attitude, the erect phallus is conspicuous by its absence from our culture. For a while we toyed with the notion of commissioning a sculpture of an erect phallus to place on the empty plinth in Trafalgar Square and filming people's reaction to it. We abandoned the idea when we realized that showing an erect penis on television is not allowed.

△ *The Divine Phallus,* first century, Pompeii.

◁ *Brennan, Pint-sized Adonis,* Ken Probst, 1996. Photographer Ken Probst's stills taken on the sets of pornographic videos have become popular collector's items.

Our attempt to reverse the legacy of the secret museum was by definition self-defeating. There is a moment in the series when a drawer containing objects from another restricted collection (the Witt Collection) was opened in the bowels of the British Museum. It was full of penises – clay amulets, bronze sculptures and other ancient artefacts – all jumbled together. It was hard not to gasp with laughter because to open a drawer and find it full of penises was so unexpected as to be surreal. But then came the revulsion, because to see all these little penises like this suggested something quite disturbing, almost demented. The collection seems an act of wilful brutality, hardly lessened by the way it had been thrown into the drawer in shameful haste. Since then I have wondered more than once if the result of our six one-hour documentaries might just perpetuate the bottom-drawer mentality of the pornographic mindset, even though our motive – to rehabilitate these images by exploring their history and social context – could hardly be more different.

Even more frustrating, our television history will inevitably serve as an electronic version of a secret museum: airing on Channel 4, a network with primary appeal to social groups A, B and C1 (the modern equivalent of 'gentlemen with appropriate demeanour'), it will be transmitted after the 9.30 p.m. watershed, a time when more men are watching and fewer women and theoretically no children. Of course, while less formal than a secret museum – ultimately anyone can watch television – it is perhaps at the same time even more restrictive. To conform with broadcast regulations, the series will, while containing full-frontal nudity, show little or no penetration or male erect members. Thus inevitably the vast majority of material that the series is about will not be shown, nor for that matter illustrated in this book!

Nevertheless, it still seemed a valuable exercise, because we have a lopsided view of the history of civilization with so much material throughout history classified as pornographic and therefore off-limits, out of reach. Furthermore, for every object preserved in a museum, secret or otherwise, countless others have been destroyed. Samuel Pepys burned his edition of *L'Ecole des Filles* after he had used it and the widow of famed explorer Sir Richard Burton, who translated many ancient erotic texts, such as the *Kamasutra* and *The Perfumed Garden*, burned a great many of his papers after his death. Because pornography's heritage has been so relentlessly destroyed and mutilated through the ages, what we are allowed to glimpse today are but the fragments of a lost history of civilization. Not long after the invention of photography, men like Henry Hayler and family, who ran a business in London's Pimlico, fled in advance of a police raid, leaving behind 130,248 prints and 5,000 negatives of sexually explicit Victorian photographs. This is a huge amount of material, considering that at the time each exposure took minutes rather than seconds and each print had to be made by hand. Today none of his work survives. Nor was Hayler alone in his endeavours. If on volume alone one were to factor in this kind of work, standard histories of photography would be a very different read.

This lost heritage suggests that, far from being a smutty sideshow, pornography has played a vital, central role in civilization. Once again the museum is the key to what that role might be. Typically, museum objects are placed on view in glass cabinets. This effects a disconnection between us and the object, sealing them off further from their past and their context. Many objects had ceremonial use or were simply everyday items that were there to be used and touched. But here, peering at these isolated objects in locked glass cases, we are rendered voyeurs, able to engage only with a gaze the intensity of which is in itself potentially pornographic.

Indeed it is this preoccupation with the hard gaze in isolation from any other activity that characterizes the modern history of pornography which might perhaps be described as 'through a glass variously'. From the glass case of the museum to the glass that frames the picture, from the lens of the camera to the movie-theatre projector, from the television screen of video to the computer screen of the digital era, the story of pornography as the story of peering at things through glass is also the story of media. It is

▷ Indian miniature from the *Kamasutra*, Jaipur school, eighteenth/ nineteenth century.

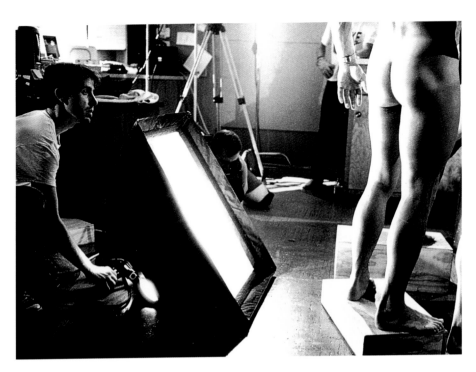

▷ *Grip Adjusts Chimera,*
Ken Probst, 1996.

the story of our obsession with inventing and using mediating technologies to help us view, probe and gaze into the very nature of things. The various lenses used, all with their own transparency, magnification and distortion, are an attempt not just to observe but also to represent. As a different way of seeing, each new mediating technology creates a different gaze with a different purpose. Pornography is the critical factor in this process because so often it was the initial application for these evolving media, helping them to refine their gaze, easing them from the margins into the mainstream. With photography, for example, audiences used to the idealized figures in nude paintings were shocked by the lumpen ugliness and artless poses of real bodies in nude photographs which also invited the label 'pornographic'. Gradually, however, people learned how to act in front of the camera, and an instrument of scientific observation became one of artistic and sexual expression. Today access to the lens – either via home video or Webcam – has become fully democratized.

The story of pornography is therefore no less than the story of the evolution of mediating technologies. Interwoven with this is also the story of the struggle to control them. From the printing press, through photography, film and video, to the computer age, each of these media is a democratizing force, giving increasing numbers of people the power of representation. At the same time, each has largely been demonized as an agent of chaos that will lead to the collapse of society unless access to it is restricted. Centuries ago it was the printing press, today it is the Internet.

Countering this social and political repression, the new technologies have found subversive power through their alliance with pornography. By definition the sexually explicit, with its emphasis on the deliberate and maximally exposed, has no respect for an establishment that depends on discretion, reserve or formal attire. Pornography shrugs off every kind of attire – literal and metaphorical – and this barefaced nakedness cannot but mock the hypocrisies and pretensions of the status quo. In short, pornography loves to masturbate in public.

This is the crux of the matter, because when the argument is stripped down to its essentials, it is possible to see that the struggle over pornography is not some genteel debate about who should be allowed to see what. It is more fundamental than that. Because pornography represents on the one hand, totally uncensored expression and, on the other (often with the other), purely unbridled pleasure, the battle over pornography is really a debate about who has the right to freedom of expression and who has the right to enjoy pleasure. Dressing this struggle up in the clothing of morality is simply a way of disguising rank élitism as righteous imperative.

Played out against such a backdrop, small wonder that what at the time seemed a harmless article in a student magazine should provoke such ugly fury. But that was almost twenty years ago and today it is more fashionable for people to fight pornography with a yawn instead of rage: 'It's so boring', 'It's all the same.' On the contrary, given pornography's focus on a specific area of human experience, it's amazing that it is so varied. However, it can't be denied that endless repetition is the beat of pornography, and in that respect it is rather like dance music, which similarly uses repetitive rhythms to work dancers into a frenzy of ecstasy. The moves may be different but the dance is the same; pleasure is the goal. It is no coincidence that the endless denunciations of such music and its scene closely parallel the criticisms of pornography. Both are described as masturbatory, as solitary and antisocial. Whether both are dismissed as boring or raged against makes little difference; the underlying critique is the same, namely that the mass pursuit of pleasure for its own sake is somehow wrong.

I believe that the outcome of the titanic struggle between pornography and the establishment is a foregone conclusion. As each new medium delivers on its democratizing promise, passing the baton to another that continues the process, there will ultimately come a point when pornography is so commonplace and such a part of everyday life that it is rendered completely unsecret and without taboo. The Internet, more than any other medium before, has delivered on this.

The Internet has also dealt a severe blow to the establishment forces used to regulating pornography. So long as it took a physical form – books, magazines, videos – pornography could always be seized and destroyed. But recently pornography has shed its physical form and gone digital. Without making windows on men's souls, it is simply not possible to monitor people's access to porn on-line. Moreover, the Internet offers the consumer not just every kind of imaginable sexual encounter, but also, while offering the solitary private masturbatory experience typical of all pornography, the opportunity to reach out and touch someone with the same rarefied interests. For example, one website lists all the parks and toilets and public places in the world where those seeking sex with men can meet. More masturbating in public! Like Alice, we step through the looking-glass of our computer screens into, if not a sexual wonderland, an 'otherland'.

If pornography is no longer a solitary masturbatory experience but a gateway to some other relationship or intercourse, if pornography was invented as a regulatory

△ One of the early photographs of nudes, an *académie, c.* 1890.

category yet can no longer be regulated, will it – at least in the form we know it – simply cease to exist?

No. Taboos and prejudices can be eroded but are rarely erased. Nevertheless, the sense of pornography as something shameful and transgressive seems to be fading.

On a balmy night in Cannes we shot the eighth annual Hot d'Or Awards. Men in black tie escorted models in couture who, just like at the Oscars, cried accepting their awards for best actress, thanking their parents, God, or their on-screen sex partner.

In New York we filmed the preview of the first major sale of ancient erotica, the Haddad family collection, at Christie's, an auction house not traditionally associated with these kinds of artefacts.

In Germany private collector Uwe Scheid unashamedly shared with us his collection of daguerreotypes of Victorian nudes which he had hitherto kept under lock and key in a bank vault.

On the outskirts of Prague we filmed American porn director Bill Higgins in a run-down barn as he shot the third in his homage to Leni Riefenstahl's *Olympiad, Prague Buddies*. Three athletes were naked and entangled with each other when the action was interrupted by the arrival of the police. The officers began barking questions about (I assumed) the ménage in front of them and I expected us all to be arrested on the spot, but abruptly they turned on their heels and left. I asked what had happened and it turned out they were not remotely worried about the perfectly legal scene in front of them. Instead they thought we might have vandalized the roof of the barn, part of which had collapsed during a storm the previous week.

Britain, however, could be relied upon to provide an exception to this mature post-porn climate of openness. Shortly after we had filmed the remains of the secret case at the British Museum, we returned to film for a documentary covering the general restoration of the museum's great courtyard. Unaccountably, we were meeting with considerable resistance on the shoot. When we finally asked why, we were told that the museum was familiar with World of Wonder as producers of pornography. Odd, but how very British, that the British Museum would penalize us for filming items in their possession, especially when, on both occasions, we were also paying for the privilege!

I am not an evangelist for what has now come to be termed 'pornography', because that would imply a belief that porn contains some moral force for good (or ill). Ultimately it has no such force. These are representations only. We invest them with voodoo powers like their ability to deprave and corrupt at our peril. (Not everyone agrees with this, and there are obvious moral complications when it comes to images created in abusive situations.) Still, a straw poll of the production team failed to yield anyone who felt that they had been depraved or corrupted by prolonged exposure to pornographic images. I doubt that anyone else believes themselves to have been depraved and corrupted by 'pornographic' images that they have seen. People who do believe that such a thing can happen generally assume it on behalf of unknown others who they imagine to be weaker or in some way less fortunate than themselves. I can almost hear them exclaim, with moral superiority, '*We* are the people who can appreciate erotica, *they* are the people who will be depraved and corrupted by pornography. Who knows, maybe they'll even start masturbating in public.'

Perhaps at the heart of all this lies a profound discomfort with our sexuality and its impenetrable mystery. No matter what laws of desire, what rules of attraction, we try to contain human sexuality within, our pursuit of sexual pleasure – in private or in public – will always at some point surprise and defy these boundaries. In the light of this, what is called for, instead of more pathologizing and moralizing, is suspension of judgement and a restored sense of wonder. Because, whether we continue to demonize it as pornography or not, there is no doubt that we will continue to employ all our arts to represent and express sexuality's essence, just as we always have.

The Road to Ruin

[Chapter One: Antiquity]

'I know it when I see it,' said US Supreme Court Justice Potter Stewart in 1964. We all know it when we see it. Whatever slipperiness pornography acquires in the courtroom or in obscure academic journals, at the end of the day it is recognizable and indisputable. Pornography may be fuzzy at the edges – fuzzy in the art gallery, fuzzy in the courtroom – but surely it is clear at the centre. People can dispute the cut-off point between the mainstream teenage magazine *19* and the niche adult magazine *Anal Teens*, but surely only the obtuse or the perverse would claim that *19* was pornographic and that *Anal Teens* was not.

There is something stubborn and irreducible about pornography that commands instant recognition. Irreducible because it has already been reduced to its limit: the body as sexual parts, sex as mechanics and hydraulics. It is in all senses stripped bare, to the core – stripped, in fact, to the hard core. For it is when sexual representation, whether in literature, photography, film or video, is deemed devoid of artistic or cultural or educational value, that it risks being judged 'obscene' in the eyes of the law.*

It is this idea that pornography stands as a hard, fixed, uncontestable, instantly recognizable thing that seduces us into thinking it is somehow outside culture. It is as though, occupying the very margins of culture, in fact the point at which culture stops, pornography could drop off the edge altogether (and good riddance, for many) and leave everything else as is.

This is precisely the notion that is disputed here, because, far from standing outside culture, independent of it, pornography is in fact a cultural construct. And while seeming to occupy the margins of culture, it is constructed at its centre – constructed at the intersections of sexuality, religion, politics, art and law. As the anthropologist

◁ This statue, from the House of the Vettii, Pompeii, once functioned as a fountain, the phallus serving as a waterspout.

---

* In the 1959 Obscene Publications Act, something is 'obscene' if, taken as a whole, it has the tendency to 'deprave and corrupt' those who are likely to come across it. There is a defence: one of public good, on the grounds that it is 'in the interests of science, literature, art or learning, or of other objects of general concern'.

▷ *Pan and the Goat* in marble, from the Villa of the Papyri, Herculaneum. When this statue was found in the mid-eighteenth century, it was hidden away with instructions that no one should have access to it.

Bernard Arcand has said, 'The history of pornography is the history of society, and nothing that happens in society can be completely left out.' [1]

Not only is pornography a cultural construct, it is a modern construct. It took the modern world with its industrializations, its technologies, and its concepts of privacy and the sanctity of the family to transform the merely sexually explicit into the new problematic category 'pornography'. Moreover, in one of pornography's many ironies, it was in the Victorian era, the period we most associate with sexual prudery, that pornography came into its own. Not just because it was then that the technology of mechanical reproduction first gave rise to the kind of material (including the photographic) that we would recognize today as pornography; not just because it was then that pornography was first produced on a scale that made it a mass phenomenon; and not just because it was then that the regulatory framework surrounding obscenity turned pornography into an industry of transgression; rather, because it was then and only then that the category of pornography itself was invented.

Despite its apparently ancient etymology – from the Greek *pornographos*, 'writing of prostitutes' the word 'pornography' was not in use before 1857. [2] Indeed, rather than being a word used by the ancient Greeks, it was virtually unknown in the classical world. There seems to be only one short passage in an ancient text where 'pornographer' makes a fleeting appearance: the *Deipnosophistae* by Athenaeus, as *pornographoi* ('whorepainters'). [3]

So it would seem to have been a relatively new word, dressed up in the garb of the old. But if it was all dressed up, did it have anywhere to go? Why the sudden need for a new word without which civilization had done perfectly well for hundreds, indeed thousands, of years?

*

The story starts in the first century AD when the water sources in the area around the Bay of Naples began to fail. Quite mysteriously, the springs and fountains had run dry, as if some deity had been displeased. It was indeed an ominous sign, but not a sign from the gods. Beneath the surface, water was evaporating into steam in the intensity of the furnace deep below. Few could have guessed what was coming next.

> . . . a portentous crash was heard, as if the mountains were tumbling in ruins; and first huge stones were hurled aloft, rising as high as the very summits, then came a great quantity of fire and endless smoke, so that the whole atmosphere was obscured and the sun was entirely hidden, as if eclipsed. Thus day was turned into night and light into darkness. Some thought that the Giants were rising again in revolt (for at this time also many of their forms could be discerned in the smoke and, moreover, a sound as of trumpets was heard), while others believed that the whole universe was being resolved into chaos or fire. [4]

These are the words of the third-century historian Dio Cassius, describing the day Vesuvius erupted, burying Pompeii in a hail of red-hot boulders, molten lava, pumice and ash, and burying neighbouring Herculaneum in a boiling sea of mud. From the time the skies went black, it would take more than sixteen hundred years for the two towns to see the light of day again, petrified as at the moment the world ended for them on 24 August 79. It was after an Italian peasant inadvertently stumbled on the ruins of Herculaneum in 1709, while digging a well, that the two sites were gradually unveiled in archaeological digs on an historic scale.

It was a unique opportunity. These were not towns that had been altered by centuries of invasions and rebuildings; artefacts whose meanings had been changed by countless hands; people whose secrets had been lost by those who followed them. Never before had there been such a chance for the modern world to survey the ancient.

It was not just the scale but the details of the finds that captured the imagination of the Western world; the evidence of human habitation was to be made even more dramatic by Giuseppe Fiorelli, head of the excavations in the latter part of the nineteenth century. It was Fiorelli who invented the technique of filling the corpse-shells made by the hardened ash with liquid plaster to re-create the final moments of Pompeii: a chained dog desperately trying to get away; a beggar dying

▽ The excavators in the eighteenth and nineteenth centuries uncovered a huge range of phallic artefacts from first-century Herculaneum and Pompeii. (Top) A drinking-bowl mask in terracotta with a tongue in shape of a phallus; (bottom) a terracotta lamp in the shape of a faun with oversized phallus; both from Pompeii.

at the Nucerian Gate; a contorted, crouching figure covering his face against the suffocating fumes.

It is difficult to overestimate the importance of the classics to the society that witnessed the unveiling of Pompeii. Classical culture, both Greek and Roman, was the cornerstone of the education system. The ancient world had become the model for civilization: the modern world was investing its future in the achievements of the past. It was as though the ancient texts from great classical civilizations would underwrite the greatness of the new ones. This did, of course, require a bit of deft footwork. It was already becoming common currency that the Roman Empire had been fatally weakened by lax morality, and concerns were expressed that parts of the classics were likely to excite the sexual feelings of young boys. None the less, with judicious selectivity it was possible to preserve society's preferred reading of ancient culture. But even the most skillful evasions would be inadequate in the face of the wholesale assault on moral sensibilities presented by the Vesuvian discoveries.

In the mid-eighteenth century, at the beginning of the excavations at Herculaneum, work started on the Villa of the Papyri, which had the largest and most impressive private collection of statuary to have survived. One statue caused immediate consternation: a marble piece of the god Pan in an apparently rewarding act of coitus with a goat. While not unfamiliar with classical references to bestiality (like Leda and the Swan), Western art had performed the singular task of keeping the sex in these images at arm's length. But whatever remoteness had been conferred upon such references was conspicuously lacking here, most notably in the detailed and meticulous rendering of the act of penetration by the phallus.

▽ A *tintinnabulum* in bronze, *The Gladiator*, from Herculaneum, discovered in 1740.

▷ Over a period of time, the phallus and testicles disappeared from illustrations of the Cerne Abbas Giant. (From top) 1764, with phallus and testicles; 1774, the phallus and most of the testicles disappear; 1842, and 1885, the phallus and testicles disappear altogether.

As Professor Andrew Wallace-Hadrill, director of the British School at Rome, says, 'Normally with a statue, the bits that you can't easily see are only roughed out. But with this, if you peer down and look in detail, you find that the genitals of both Pan and the nanny goat are fully present and visible. You can't ever get an uninterrupted view, you must always look through a haze of legs and hoofs, but they're there all right.'[5]

In a response that telescopes any distance we have travelled from the eighteenth and nineteenth centuries to today, the statue seemingly still has the power to shock. When John Paul Getty re-created the Villa of the Papyri later in the twentieth century, although he reproduced most of its significant garden statuary, the Pan and the Goat was omitted, despite the fact that it is one of the finest pieces of the collection.[6]

In the past, as in recent times, the immediate impulse was to hide it from view. Charles of Bourbon, King of Naples and Sicily, gave orders that the statue be entrusted to the care of the royal sculptor, Joseph Canart, with specific instructions that no one should have access to it.

But the shock of the old did not end there. Unearthed from the ruins was a giant phallus in painted tufa that stood over two feet tall. There were the drinking-bowl masks, the mouths of which, instead of tongues, had phalluses which would bob around in the bowl when it was full. There was a terracotta lamp in the shape of a faun with an oversized veined phallus with detailed glans. There were flying phalluses with tiny wings and dangling bells.

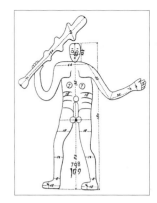

The age that unearthed this profusion of phalluses was the age that had eliminated the phallus from view. If, as was becoming apparent, the phallus was everywhere in ancient Rome, it was nowhere in the eighteenth and nineteenth centuries. This, and increasingly so, was a delicate and genteel age. As a writer in the *Gentleman's Magazine* of 1791 remarked, 'We are every day becoming more delicate, and without doubt, at the same time, more virtuous; and shall, I am confident, become the most refined and polite people in the world.'[7] And while later in England, contrary to popular belief, Victorians might not in fact have seen the need to hide piano legs in crinolines (based, as this idea was on a single, unverifiable observation by an Englishman in America, recounted only to ridicule[8]), this was certainly an age that witnessed a refinement of language from the latter part of the eighteenth century, not only in England but also in Europe and in the United States, where legs were to be referred to as 'limbs' and chicken breasts as chicken 'bosoms'. But this delicacy of language served only to draw attention to and sexualize hitherto undreamed of and unheeded sexual territory.

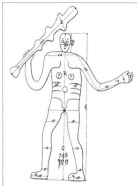

These were not the first ancient phalluses to demand attention from those who would have preferred to ignore them. The Cerne Abbas Giant presented an impressive example on the North Dorset Downs. It is still not known when he was etched into the chalk as there is no record of him prior to 1694, when churchwardens' accounts dated 4 November refer to a payment 'for repairing of ye Giant 3s 0d.'[9] Nor is it clear what he represented: was this a Roman Hercules, part of a short-lived cult advanced by Emperor Commodus; or an image of Helis the Huntsman, an Iron Age god or warrior; or even, as is sometimes suggested, a practical joke?[10]

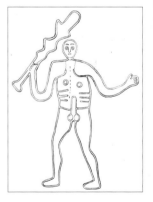

Whatever his origins, though, the Cerne Abbas Giant was a troubling presence in the eighteenth and nineteenth centuries. The first known illustration appeared in 1764 in the *Gentleman's Magazine*, complete with genitals. However, mysteriously the penis had dropped off by the time of the next known illustration, in 1774, while the testicles had been reduced to two large boil-like objects on the inner thighs. By the Victorian era, both the penis and the testicles had disappeared from illustrations altogether.[11] And nature imitated art when the giant member was gradually covered by a fig leaf of overgrown grass. When it was proposed by Lord Rivers that the giant be cleaned up again, the vicar of Cerne Abbas expressed concern that this would have an undesirable effect on the morals of his parishioners. In 1868, when the cleaning took place with apparently restorative effects on the giant member, one observer commented 'In the sequestered valley…the eye is arrested by the apparition of a gigantic human figure …which…is an astounding and probably a repulsive object…As to the anatomical proportions of the relative parts of his frame we prefer to remain silent.'*[12]

---

* Quaint as this may seem today, while top-shelf magazines regularly show, in great detail, splayed female genitalia, the erection or otherwise of the penis still serves as an effective dividing line for magazine editors between what is and what is not acceptable for general sale. The erect penis is still a hallmark of obscenity, and to show it is to run the risk of seizure under the Obscene Publications Act. It is this that still confines the legal beefcake magazines to the partially erect penis. Exactly where to draw the line is a trickier question, however, and acceptable levels of engorgement are the subject of some discussion.

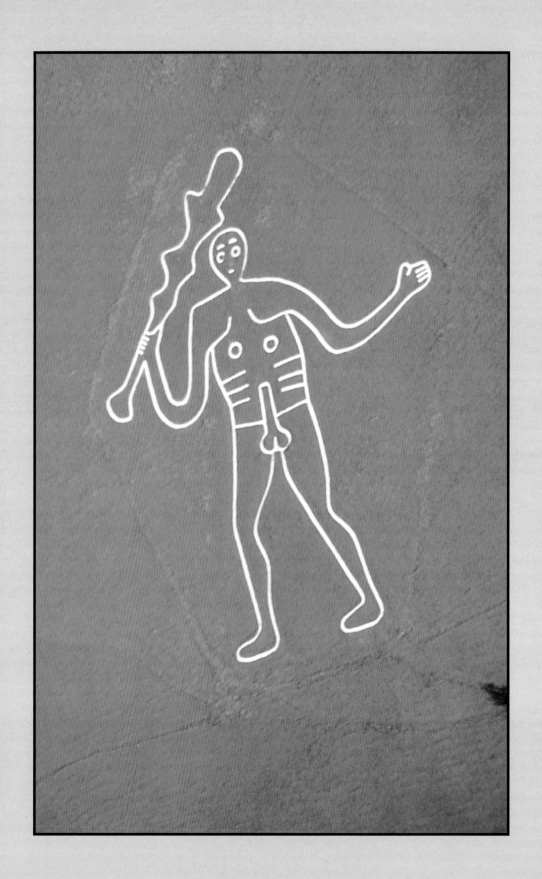

The sheer quantity of phallic objects being unearthed at Pompeii and Herculaneum was mesmerizing: 'For the very first time we had a whole town, a whole culture, and it was possible to see where that imagery fitted into the town. And for the first time it became impossible to avoid the fact that on every street corner you could see an erect phallus,'[13] explains Cambridge classicist, Dr Simon Goldhill.

These outrageous artefacts presented a problem to the excavators. Public display was out of the question, as the objects were clearly unfit for exhibition, and yet, in the interests of archaeology, haphazard as that nascent science was, the objects could not be destroyed. The excavators ultimately took the only course of action available to them. As with the Pan and the Goat statue, they hid them away. Following a suggestion by Francis I, Duke of Calabria, in 1819 that the erotic artefacts should be confined to a single room in the Museum of Naples, so that access could be limited to 'persons of mature age and of proven morality', more than a hundred objects were confined to the so-called Gabinetto degli Oggetti Osceni (Cabinet of Obscene Objects).

As Walter Kendrick has so effectively argued, the nineteenth century had risen to the cultural challenge of the erotic onslaught from the ancient Romans by creating a brand-new physical and cultural space: a 'secret museum'. This was a place that would preserve both knowledge and public morality; a place where problematic objects could be separated and set aside, with access restricted and monitored. And a new name was found for these objects: 'pornography'. The first official, systematic catalogue of this collection appeared in 1866, and it was simply called the 'Pornographic Collection'.[14]

The etymology of the word 'obscene' is unclear. Some suggest the origin is the Latin *ob caenum*, 'from filth'. Others favour the Latin *ob scena*, meaning 'off or to one side of the stage'. Lynda Nead is among the latter, suggesting, therefore, that the secret museum can be seen as a spatial enactment of the term 'obscene'.[15] The objects themselves were made to act out their own obscenity by being carted off-scene, out of view and beyond presentation. The secret museum was at once part of the museum yet separated off from it. While its presence was not denied, the museum would act as if it was not there. Like the annexation of sex in the society that created the secret museum, it was both there and not there; part of society and yet not properly acknowledged.

Classical culture was the heritage of the nineteenth century; people had fashioned themselves in its image. How could the image of classical (and therefore contemporary) society be rescued in the light of these new discoveries? 'It's very important for the Victorians that the ancient world, both Greek and Roman, was full of clean white statues that they could respond to as purity, beauty and sublimity. The discovery of extensive works that they thought obscene caused a problem. They had to sustain their image in the face of what was really quite stunning counter-evidence and one of the ways they did it was by inventing a category of the obscene which they could segregate off, separate to one side in secret museums; they could say that it is some area of ancient culture but not the ancient culture which provides us with its inheritance,' says Simon Goldhill.

Having created a secret museum, the next question was who should have access to it – or rather, who should not have access to it. The special Pornographic Collection was kept in a locked room. Admission was restricted to those with a valid royal permit and later, after Giuseppe Garibaldi assumed power, by special permission of the directors of

◁ The Cerne Abbas Giant, on the North Dorset Downs.

the museum. Women, children and the lower classes were all excluded; pornography was to be the preserve of the educated gentleman.

'The gentleman,' says Simon Goldhill, 'considered himself to be protected from erotic stimulation and corruption. If you were a proper gentleman, you were above the possibilities of that sort of corruption. It was only the vulnerable, the women and the children and the working classes, who might be corrupted by this.' Position and power were preserved by this act of keeping certain groups out, allowing gentlemen who were granted access to reaffirm their social status and power.

The fear stalking the age was any loss of control that might threaten the very roots of social order and empire; good order in the family and among the lower classes was held to be fundamental. Women in particular were thought to be weak and vulnerable and in need of protection from sexual material; but equally, the fear was that they would be rendered dangerous and troublesome if they were excited by it. What posed as an act of protection should perhaps more accurately be seen as an act of self-protection. As Simon Goldhill remarks, 'This is fear of female sexuality. Female sexuality threatened the very substance of society. Female sexual pleasure at one level threatened the security of marriage; the security of the family and children and childbirth and legitimacy. At another level it threatened the security of the men themselves and their own self-identity; the fear and threat to the male identity of female sexual pleasure.'

△ Nineteenth-century guidebook illustrations of the Pornographic Collection in Naples cut out, covered, or changed the shape of the phallus. (César Famin from his 'Royal Museum at Naples' guide, *c*.1871.)

In addition, children and males of immature years would need to be kept out of the secret museum. Once again, the fear was the corrupting influence of inappropriate sexual material. Indeed, warnings about the calamitous fate of the habitual self-abuser whipped up a state of sufficient anxiety to create a market for penile rings with spikes to deflate unwitting ardour during sleep and, even more terrifying, a device whereby a filial erection was made to ring an electric bell in the parents' room! 'Self-indulgence, long pursued, tends ultimately, if carried far enough, to early death or self-destruction,' declared William Acton in his book *The Function and Disorders of the Reproductive Organs*, which was published in 1857 and ran to four editions in his lifetime. This was Acton's description of a habitual masturbator:

The frame is stunted and weak, the muscles undeveloped, the eye is sunken and heavy, the complexion is sallow, pasty, or covered with spots of acne, the hands are damp and cold, and the skin moist. The boy shuns the society of others, creeps about alone, joins with repugnance in the amusements of his schoolfellows. He cannot look any one in the face, and becomes careless in dress and uncleanly in person. His intellect has become sluggish and enfeebled, and if his evil habits are persisted in, he may end in becoming a drivelling idiot or a peevish valetudinarian. Such boys are to be seen in all stages of degeneration, but what we have described is but the result towards which they all are tending. [16]

The fact that this was a ruinous pit into which anyone – indeed everyone – could fall makes it more than an issue for the individual; it was an issue for society.

Girls were equally at risk, according to Samuel-Auguste-André-David Tissot's *Onanism: Essay on the Ailments Produced by Masturbation*, first published in 1758. [17] Masturbation in females could lead finally to 'uterine fury, which deprives them at once of modesty and reason and puts them on the level of the lewdest brutes, until a despairing death snatches them away from pain and infamy'.

Even after creating a secret museum, there was the problem of how to record its contents. In an age of obsessive classification, how would these objects be listed? With difficulty, as it turned out, and authors of guidebooks and catalogues were impaled on the horns of yet another dilemma: should they serve good taste or truth?

On the whole, it was truth that lost out. Phalluses were either lopped off completely, covered with fig leaves or tapered into improbable cones. Clouding over the especially rude bits turned out to be a particularly useful way of saving the blushes of illustrator and reader alike. One catalogue resorted to the use of untranslated Latin and Greek to allow the author to assure all concerned that proper care had been taken to keep unsuitable material out of the wrong hands: 'We have taken all the prudential measures applicable to such a collection of engravings and text. We have endeavoured to make its reading inaccessible, so to speak, to poorly educated persons, as well as those whose sex and age forbid any exception to the laws of decency and modesty.' [18]

The statue of *Pan and the Goat* presented a special problem. Gelding it could not efface the bestial and unacceptable whole, so it was either left out altogether and simply not listed or accompanied by a health warning. One catalogue, after taking the precaution of clouding over the genitals, exhorts the reader to 'turn the page over quickly'.

The confusion and uncertainty about the best way of dealing with these shocking artefacts were mirrored in the apparent arbitrariness of the treatment of some of the objects themselves, particularly in the early years of excavation. Of the five pictures that you can see today on the south wall of the tavern on the Street of Mercury in Pompeii, two have been defaced beyond recognition; the same is true of two pictures on the east wall. Our only knowledge of the original sexual content of these paintings comes via surviving engravings by Roux, published in 1836. [19] As the images that have not survivied are those with an

▽ Herculaneum and Pompeii catalogue illustrations, 1840. Illustrations were often fogged or roughly sketched to preserve modesty.

erotic content, it seems likely that they were destroyed in some act of moral outrage. Sometimes, in an ironic reversal of moral fortunes, the very survival of the obscenity is due to an excess of moral zeal. For instance, in the House at IX.5.16 a small room containing erotic pictures is the one best preserved, whereas the rest of the building and those surrounding it are in ruins. The only reason this room is still intact today, according to art historian Professor John Clarke, is because a solid roof and heavy door were built by the excavators to 'protect the morals of the curious'. [20]

It was known, of course, that erotic artefacts had been made in ancient Greece and Rome; they had been thrown up on a piecemeal basis for centuries. What shocked the excavators was their ubiquity. 'It was all right to find one, but to find so many made them think that this must have been a world turned upside down, where every value that these gentlemen had was completely cancelled out by the hideous obscenity of life that they were uncovering,' says John Clarke.[21]

This was not the Roman Empire people either expected or wanted to find, and attempts to understand the ancient in terms of the modern proved an unexpected trial. The sexual practices and associated imagery of the ancients were being nailed to the Procrustean bed of Victorianism and, not surprisingly, they did not fit. Stretched to breaking point, something had to give. The first casualty was understanding.

Revealing their own prejudices about the display of sexual material in public spaces, early excavators reasoned that all erotic paintings and artefacts must belong to a brothel if they could not easily be placed in a quasi-religious category. In 1780 when Pierre Sylvain Maréchal catalogued certain vases, lamps and everyday utensils, he noted, 'We must believe that articles shaped like this were intended only for bawdyhouses,'[22] so inconceivable would be the depravity otherwise.

For the age that uncovered these obscenities, following the logic of the story of the

▽ (Left) Male-female couple performing sexual acrobatics, from the inn on the Street of Mercury, Pompeii: these engravings (after Barré, 1827) are the only means we have of knowing the content of some of the paintings that have been destroyed. (Right) One of the original defaced sex scenes on the south wall of the inn on the Street of Mercury.

◁ Woman wearing a breast band, crouching over a man, from the House of the Centenary, Pompeii.

Fall in Christian tradition (at least as it had been handed down), innocence = sexual innocence = lack of sexual knowledge. But inherent in this reasoning there is a flaw, because once innocence and guilt are hitched to knowledge, it becomes impossible to recognize innocence without having lost it oneself. The ability to name the guilty simply underlines one's own lack of innocence, like the dirty-minded censor who sees smut everywhere. There is a logical impossibility at the heart of Western tradition. What, then, was the solution to this double-bind? The solution was hypocrisy. Some Victorian ladies, for instance, felt obliged to swoon when confronted with the sexually suggestive – an act that was at once a private recognition of and a public refusal to admit what one had seen or heard. Sex was alluded to but not named. Sex was present but not acknowledged.

▷ Man and woman on a bed, with attendant, from the House of Caecilius Lucundus.

This was a society whose policing and management of the sexual were compartmentalized in the extreme. According to one book of etiquette dated 1863, it was even supposedly desirable that works of male and female authors 'unless they happen to be married'[23] should be separated on bookshelves. The hypocritical nature of Victorian society can be overstated, but, without wishing to oversimplify or be blinded by what Peter Gay has called the 'hardy commonplaces that have so long obstructed our view',[24] it is clear that the society that instituted segregated sexuality in its own Christian world was the same society that erroneously assumed it in the pre-Christian world. Looking through the wrong end of the historical and conceptual telescope, the only approach available to them was their own compartmentalized and sexualized world view.

Out of the frying pan and into the fire. The automatic designation 'brothel' for anything that displayed sexual imagery gave rise to some unusual statistics. It meant that

Pompeii would have had thirty-five brothels, a striking per capita concentration of one brothel for seventy-one men and nearly eighty times as many brothels per capita as Rome![25] 'It's ridiculous. In fact Pompeii had only one building that was actually made for the purpose, and the rest of them were inventions of the dirty minds of the "Victorians". Every time they saw something that looked like sex, they wanted to name it a brothel,' says John Clarke.[26]

Take, for instance, the House of the Centenary, which takes up a whole block and obviously belonged to a wealthy family. In a small room there are two erotic paintings: one shows a woman astride a man with her back to him and the other a woman with a 'breast band' crouching over the man and seemingly guiding his penis. According to John Clarke, those who discovered this room, and rooms like it in Pompeii, reasoned it must be a brothel, part of the house that had gone 'bad'. 'Everyone wanted to make it into a brothel when it was discovered in the nineteenth century. There is no other way it could be explained in their terms. But in fact this is a luxurious room in a very luxurious house.'

The next assumption was that the room must be some kind of chamber reserved especially for lovemaking. Wrong again, according to Clarke. The key to understanding the significance of the pictures in Pompeii is to understand their original context. Where were they seen? Who would have seen them? Where did they belong in the house? In this context, he argues, a proper consideration of the layout of the house shows that this little room can be seen as an entertainment suite, imitating similar suites in wealthy villas. It spelled 'luxury', not 'lust'. 'It's the place that the patron would have brought his favourite and most important guests', says Clarke. 'The images were to make people understand that the owner had good taste. They were not to turn people on. There was no notoriety. It was a matter of showing the beautiful aspects of sexual play. It was sex as sport.'

What confounded the excavators in their attempt to understand first-century Romans was as much their concepts of privacy as their ideas about sex. 'There is no word for privacy in the Latin language. There's no way to express it. There are places where you can be secret, but that's always for some sort of political activity. It's not for sex,' according to Clarke. Simon Goldhill says, 'It's very striking that as soon as the images were discovered on Pompeiian walls they were all assumed to be in the most private rooms of the houses. But we now know that many of these images were indeed in the most public spaces of Roman culture. Public and private are not natural divisions. Cultures divide them differently: for Victorians in particular, their close commitment to privacy and pornography is quite different from a Roman sense of the public performance of your own identity.'

The Victorians had not expected to find these pictures on open display. 'It was very perplexing, because what they wanted to do was to find them only in dark, dirty corners where people did it. And instead what it shows is that people were proud of them. They wanted to show them to the people that came to see them in their houses. These were proper pictures to have in their house,' says John Clarke.

The infamous *Pan and the Goat* statue was openly displayed in the peristyle garden of the Villa of the Papyri at Herculaneum. Not only was it evidently acceptable to the wealthy owner of his house but it would have been seen by respectable visitors, and

was on show with statues that had no discernible sexual content at all. It is clear that what the modern world found imperative to remove from view was, to the ancients, natural enough to display in the house. As Andrew Wallace-Hadrill says, 'These Roman images show us the sexual just naturally inhabiting all sorts of areas. They may be displayed in the garden, in general circulation areas, and one reason for that is they don't think of the house as this place for the family.'

Children had access to these images, as did women. 'What everyone wanted to find, and they didn't find,' according to John Clarke, 'is that somehow the Romans cordoned off these paintings from the children and from the women. And the [excavators] tried to find passages in the ancient literature which would say this, and you have to look very hard to find even one prude who said, well, maybe young girls shouldn't be looking at pictures of copulation. Ridiculous. Children, women, people of every class saw and enjoyed these images.'

The Roman state may not have attempted to regulate sexual images, but this did not mean that there were no rules of sexual behaviour. Ideas about what was proper were deeply etched in the Roman psyche.

At the risk of oversimplification, the basic sexual rule for the Romans was to penetrate but not be penetrated. It did not much matter who you did it to, how you did it, what orifice you chose to enter by; the cardinal point was to screw and not be screwed. Sex being what it is and requiring at least two, someone was always on the wrong end of the deal: women, slaves, prostitutes, young males and even children. Penetration was a way of expressing masculine citizenship; to be a proper citizen you had to be a penetrating, active male. As John Clarke says, 'As long as the man is involved in inserting his penis, it doesn't matter too much in what part of the other person he is inserting it. As long as he maintains his phallic position, he is completely without shame.'

According to Simon Goldhill, 'The threat of passivity was the threat that you lost self-control, that you became the object of somebody else's desire. In the ancient world, desire is something very rarely reciprocal. You don't want to be loved back by someone you love. That's a modern invention. For the Roman citizen, you should desire somebody and not be the object of desire. You had to be the master of your body and its desires. The worst thing that could happen is that you become the object of somebody else's mastery or desires. That is to say, a slave, or indeed a woman. Hence being penetrated or even, at an extreme, being desired makes you not the subject, not the master of your own being.'

In short, the principles of appropriate sexual behaviour centred on the notion of the Roman male citizen and what was required to maintain his status. Sexuality, like much else in Roman society, was based on inequality and power; and the social position of the freeborn male was expressed in the act of sex.

In 1986 a set of paintings was discovered in a changing room of a complex of Roman baths known as the Suburban Baths, so called because they stood just outside Pompeii's walls. The Suburban Baths had a number of attractions: a dry-heat room, a large heated swimming pool, a cold plunge, a mosaic waterfall and a number of elaborately decorated rooms. And in the middle of these was the changing room, with a sequence of the most sexually explicit images to be found in the whole of Pompeii.

◁ (Top) Threesome of two men and a woman in the changing room of the Suburban Baths, Pompeii (image V1). (Bottom) A man performing cunnilingus on a woman (image IV) in the changing room of the Suburban Baths, Pompeii. These paintings (AD62–79) were on open view to all who attended these luxurious baths.

▷ The Warren Cup, a first-century Roman drinking cup: two males on a mattress. The older man penetrates the younger male.

They were painted directly above a series of two-dimensional painted 'boxes', which in turn represent real lockers below (these have now disappeared) where bathers would have deposited their clothes. Each of the painted 'boxes' has a number so that (presumably) each sexual image, plus its 'box', represented the real locker below it. The image above box number III shows fellatio – a relatively rare image in Roman paintings, as it was a sexual practice primarily associated with prostitutes. Box number IV's image shows cunnilingus, as the woman spreads her legs and exposes her depilated genitalia. Images of cunnilingus are even rarer than those of fellatio, and this one is unique among wall paintings that have survived. The image attached to box number VI depicts a threesome: one man penetrates another man, who in turn penetrates a woman. The image for box VII shows four people having sex.[27]

The Suburban Baths are not divided into separate sections for men and women. There is only one dressing room and it is thought to have been used by both sexes: 'Every man and woman who would come to the baths would see these as he or she undressed and got ready to bathe and exercise,' says Clarke. Even more significant is the fact that the sexual acts depicted would have been considered improper at the time. Many of these were acts that were not appropriate for a Roman citizen to engage in. For here, not

◁ Naples Museum,
c.1890.

only were the sexual acts those associated with prostitutes, but in many cases the man is seen in passive sexual positions which would have considerably compromised his active, penetrative status as a Roman male citizen. These were images that turned social etiquette upside down. Even so, they were not the object of the sorts of furtive, hidden glances that have come to characterize pornography today. They were available and openly witnessed – and presumably enjoyed – in a public space. 'For us it's almost impossible to imagine having representations of sex that we would call hard-core in a place where we would also bathe, socialize, perhaps listen to a concert, exercise and so on,' continues Clarke. 'It's completely inconceivable to us moderns to have that kind of mixture of sexual imagery of such an outrageous sort in a place where you do normal innocent socializing.'

Naples did not house the only secret museum in Europe. Other collections of pornography existed in Florence, Dresden and Madrid in private galleries which acted as depositories for 'obscene relics' brought from Egypt and Greece. London too had its own Museum Secretum, which was started in 1865 when the British Museum accepted a collection of erotic objects from George Witt. The curators of the British Museum were faced with the same dilemma as their Neapolitan counterparts, and their solution ran along similar lines. As Dr David Gaimster, curator of medieval and later antiquities at the British Museum, says, 'It was forbidden to destroy the material culture of the past; at the same time, it was forbidden to display the objects. So access to the Secretum was tightly controlled. Those persons wishing to see the collections would write to the director of the museum or the head keeper to apply to see this material, and then would have

undergone a stringent cross-examination. The process was calculated to weed out all but the most scholarly and the most honest.'[28]

In the secret museum in Naples, any item of an apparently sexual nature, whether it was religious, apotropaic or symbolic, was dumped in this one place, creating a peculiar repository of orphaned objects. There are small phallus amulets that were hung around a child's neck – little more than good-luck charms, like horseshoes today; phalluses from household shrines; marble sculptures from Roman art collections designed to show off the wealth and good taste of their owners; decorative bronzes; and votive phallic carvings designed as offerings for the gods. There are functional everyday household objects like lamps and vases and mirrors; *lebes* or basins that were used in religious rituals; *tintinnabula* or phalluses with bells to ward off the 'evil eye'; paintings that had been hacked down from walls. These are things that do not belong together, but once put side by side and classified as dirty, naughty, rude, the label tends to stick. As Catherine Johns of the British Museum says, 'The different classes of sexual representation had a wide range of meanings, and . . . *none* of them, in antiquity, would have aroused the furtive, guilty and hostile response which they have *all* been accorded in the recent past.'[29]

The oddity of the secret museum is apparent today. According to John Clarke, 'What they were creating when they made these pornographic collections was the equivalent of a modern sex shop. What it does, of course, is it creates a concentration that totally distorts the context that these came from.'

At the beginning of the nineteenth century 'obscenity' began to be the consideration that overrode all others in deciding how to classify objects of the past. Items with any kind of sexual content were separated out, compartmentalized and hidden away. And

△ Greek red-figure cup by the Brygos painter *c.* 480BC. In the ancient world, sexual imagery was not confined to Roman artefacts. Scenes of intercourse and fellatio were common in Greek painted pottery, especially on the *kylix*, or drinking cup, used at the symposium.

◁ Priapus weighing his phallus against a sack of money, from the House of the Vetii, Pompeii.

▷ A Roman marble relief
of Hercules and a nymph,
c. AD 150. Hercules' club
rests to the right, against a
pedestal carrying a figure
of the phallic god Priapus.

then they were misunderstood. No matter where the objects had come from, no matter what purpose they had served, they were automatically labelled obscene. Removed from their original contexts, they were grouped under the new and artificial heading 'obscenity', which, as Catherine Johns points out, 'is not a scholarly category, it is a moral one, and it is academically indefensible'.[30] Once torn from the context that gave them meaning, their significance was often lost altogether. It was an injury whose mark scholarship bears to this day.

The remnants of Europe's secret museums can still be seen, often retained from a sense of nostalgia. After the Second World War, as attitudes changed, many of the objects – at the British Museum, for example – emerged from their cupboards to join the public collections. But not every object. As David Gaimster says, 'There was a sense that perhaps it would be important to try to maintain this collection to provide scholars and interested observers with a nineteenth-century time capsule.'

The moral logic that created the secret museum is today derided rather than shared. In fact, there's nothing like a shot of Victorian moralizing to confirm our own sense of superiority. We use the Victorians to feel better about ourselves. But as the walls of the secret museums have been dismantled by a more liberal age, the secret museums still stand. These days we may not furnish them with the same objects – a century of legal

◁ Seated man fondling a boy, depicted on the interior of a Greek red-figure cup, *c.* 480–470BC.

wrangling over the meaning of 'obscenity' has put paid to that. Religious and artistic artefacts have been rescued from the dark and naughty corner and put back on open display. But a category of objects we wish to separate out, hide away, keep from view, worry over and police still exists. And we still call those objects by the same name: 'pornography'.

As Andrew Wallace-Hadrill says, 'Inescapably we are the heirs of our Victorian ancestors. The moment you set up the category of the pornographic, the moment you say that area is separate from and different from everything else, you can change the internal rules that define pornography as much as you like, but it will still remain separate. Separate in a way that wasn't true of the Roman world.'

In one fell swoop, the secret museum had created a new problematic category which was deemed dangerous and morally threatening – a threat which would require policing if society was to be protected. This legacy is still with us, and indeed is part of a much larger inheritance. Having invented the term 'sexuality', this was an age that created hitherto unknown pathologies and unimagined deviancies of sexual behaviour. The pornographic was but a product of this new taxonomy of sex. But while 'pornography' as a regulatory category may have been invented in the nineteenth century, this is not when the story of the problem of sexual representation starts. For this we must turn to what happened during the hundreds of years that passed between the burying of Pompeii and its eventual excavation: the triumph of Christianity.

The Sacred and Profane

I n one of the many ironies that litter its history, the foundation stone for the very creation of pornography as we know it was laid by Christianity. As the Roman Empire faltered in the late fourth and early fifth centuries, Christianity was already taking the Western world on a novel path. In this new Christian world, sex would be framed by a new language: the language of sin.

All societies attempt to control sex in some way, but it was Christianity that opted to do so by loading it with such a heavy moral freight. Under Christianity, sex was not just another moral problem, it became *the* moral problem. It was when sex and sexual pleasure became dirty, shameful and sinful that their representations were seen as problematic – ob-scene, off scene, something to be hidden away. In fact, if sexual pleasure had not become so problematic in the first place, it is hard to see how the category 'pornography' would have been created at all.

The Church became the ultimate arbiter of what was and was not considered off limits, and the very act of judgement created and populated the category of the sexually obscene. So Christianity had a profound impact not only on the way we talk about pornography (bad/smutty/dirty/degrading) but also on its very nature. If pornography today is recognizable (and, according to some, definable) as the separation of sex from the rest of human experience, it was Christianity that effected that divorce. If pornography today is known by the reduction of sex to bodily mechanics and hydraulics, it was Christianity that stripped the soul out of it. If pornography today is shadowed by private guilt and public scorn, it was Christianity that sought from its earliest years to police sex by private confession and public disavowal. And, finally, if pornography today is tagged by a sense of danger and threat, it was Christianity that invested sex and sexual representation with the power of subversion.

Right from the start the body was considered the enemy of the soul. St Augustine of Hippo (354–430) was echoing St Paul when he said, 'Walk in the Spirit, and ye shall not fulfil the lust of the flesh; for the flesh lusteth against the Spirit, and the Spirit against the flesh; and these are contrary the one to the other.'[1] The body was despised and scorned.

◁ Detail from *The Garden of Earthly Delights* (*c*.1516) by Hieronymous Bosch. Christianity in the Middle Ages presented pleasures of the flesh as part of the chaos of the Fall, ultimately leading to damnation.

Pope Innocent III (1160–1216) would see in spit, urine and excrement the 'vile ignobility of human existence'; to the medieval Christian, all were born 'between shit and piss'.

When it came to sex, it was St Augustine more than any other who stamped his views on the Church. Not unfamiliar with the pleasures of the flesh himself, he embraced Christianity in 386 and renounced his past with all the fanaticism of the convert. Condemning, as he did in the second book of his *Confessions*, the 'past foulness, and the carnal corruptions' of his soul when 'he walked the streets of Babylon and wallowed in its mire',[2] he developed the view that sex as we know it (like hard labour, pain in childbirth and death) was part of God's punishment for Original Sin, Adam and Eve's disobedience in the Garden of Eden. While a pure form of sex existed in Paradise, the sex drive, the passions that go with sex, he thought, were absent. Sexual desire, a depraved craving, was the very badge of the Fall from Grace and marriage nothing but a 'legalised depravity'.[3] There was no glory here, only abjection. But if sex was the consequence of turning away from God, to renounce sex was to turn back to Him.[4]

In the new Christian age, sex got in the way of God: sexual demons, lustful women, treacherous Eves – all beckoned to a Godless future of death and damnation. Better not to touch a woman at all;[5] better to be a eunuch for the sake of the kingdom of heaven.[6] Celibacy was best. It was this profoundly negative view of sex that came to dominate the mindset of the Church, as the celibate clergy, with their claims to superior spiritual and moral status, eventually consolidated their power and secured positions of leadership, setting in motion a process that would problematize sex and sexual representation to the present day.

*

When Christianity changed from a persecuted minority to an established majority religion in the fourth and fifth centuries, solitary monks had already taken to the desert in pursuit of their own brand of asceticism. They chastised and mortified their bodies for the sake of their souls. And in these self-imposed experiments in abstinence, it was the sexual urges that troubled them the most. Making the renunciation of sex their chief imperative, they were often dismayed to find that their bodies betrayed them with involuntary erections and wet dreams. Different monks took revenge on their recalcitrant flesh in different ways, burning themselves with red-hot irons, or holding asps and cold metal to their genitals.[7]

Chased from the body, sex fled into the mind. By subduing the body by force, they were tortured by desire. The repression of sex only led to an obsession with sex, and as the individual monks turned away from their desert isolation and formed themselves into communities, their rules betrayed this obsession. Pachomius (290–347) was the founder of the first great monasteries in Egypt, and there was a pervasive sense of sexual danger in the monastic rules and exhortations. According to one set of their precepts, monks were required to cover their knees when sitting together, avoid tucking up their tunics too high when washing clothes together and keep each other at arm's length; they were forbidden to bathe together or apply ointments to each other, to be alone in pairs and to talk to each other in the dark.[8] In taking every precaution to remove temptations of the flesh, monastic life was dominated by temptations of the flesh: the organization and daily timetable were about sex, sex, sex! Individual monks may not have talked sex, but institutionally they shouted it.

▷ Drawing by Borel and engraving by Elluin for *Thérèse Philosophe*, attributed to Diderot, 1785. The confessor who derives sexual pleasure from both the confession and the punishment became a familiar theme in transgressive imagery in the Christian West.

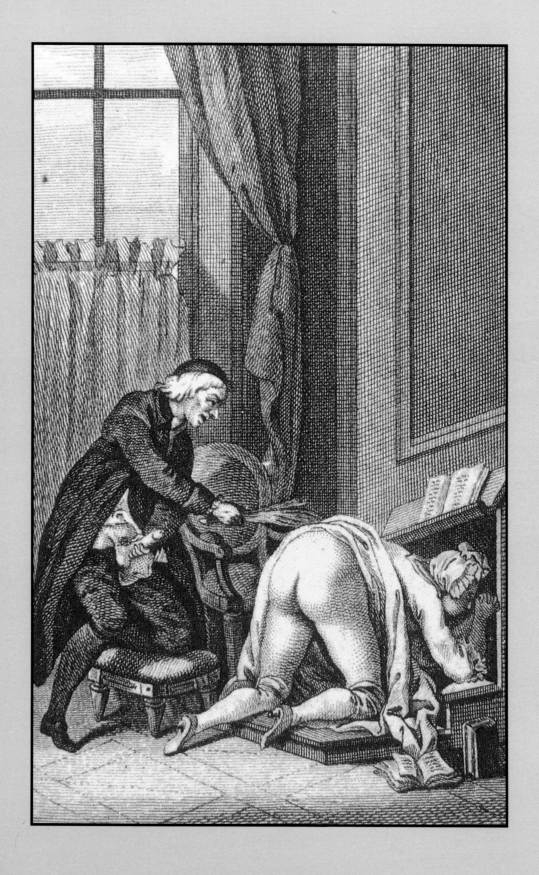

The fevered antipathy to sex could be barbaric. As a virgin bride of Christ, a nun could stray from the path only at the expense of becoming an adulteress against Christ – an insult to God that on occasion provoked severe punishment. In one episode in the twelfth century a nun from the convent of Watton in Yorkshire took a lover and fell pregnant. Once discovered, in their zeal to avenge the wrongdoing, fellow nuns took her lover, held him down and forced her to castrate him. The severed organ, 'befouled with blood', was then rammed into her mouth.[9]

For ordinary folk who were unable or unwilling to take the higher path of chastity, a system of sexual rules, regulations and enforcements was developed that was no less obsessive. From the beginning of the seventh century, guidelines for acceptable sexual behaviour were spelled out in the so-called penitentials and other handbooks for confessors, and the most intimate details of married life were opened up for examination and judgement in the canonical courts and confessionals. The penitential writers detailed the days of the week a married couple could have sex (not Wednesdays, Fridays or Sundays), how they could have sex (not naked, not from behind, not with the woman on top, not anally, not orally or lustfully), when they could have sex (not during menstruation, pregnancy, nursing or daylight hours) and who could not have sex (the unmarried, men together, oneself alone).[10] In other words, temperate heterosexual relations in the missionary position for the purposes of procreation within marriage and in the dark. Anything else was a sin, and as such could even be pursued through the courts. Ordinary people found at fault by the canonical courts could expect a fine and sometimes a humiliating public confession and whipping.[11]

Flagellation as a means of punishment and atonement for sins of the flesh acquired a peculiar pyscho-sexual significance in the Western tradition, and would appear and reappear in pornographic imagery through the centuries. The confessor who derives sexual pleasure from not only the sexual confession but also the punishment is a familiar stereotype in obscene works. According to Catherine Johns, who made a study of erotica in Greece and Rome, flagellation is virtually absent as an erotic motif in Greek and Roman art (apart from some slipper-

△ Cartoon of Lord Longford, from the *Daily Mail*, 11 August 1971. Critics, censors and investigators of pornography occupy unstable ground as they are also its consumers.

wielding in Greek pottery) and yet is a recurrent motif in later Western imagery – particularly in the more repressive Victorian era. As she remarks, 'Perhaps one should conclude that a repressive attitude to sexuality is particularly conducive to this taste, combining pleasure and punishment in a way which satisfies both the desire and the guilt.'[12]

The confessional was the first arena for controlling the dark dangers of sex, and priests were encouraged to be diligent and thorough in their examination of the penitent's sexual behaviour. The codification of the sacrament of penance by the Lateran Council in 1215 prompted the development of a range of confessional techniques, and a confessional culture requiring even greater awareness of the sins of the body.

The writer and philosopher Michel Foucault has argued that the Western tradition systematically turns sex into 'discourse', controlling sex by a continuous exhortation to speak about it and turn it into 'knowledge'. The willingness to talk about sex, to explore it, to write about it, to enter into therapy about it, to conduct scientific surveys about it and even to make television series about it does not signify some brave new world of sexual revolution that started in the 1960s and breaks in some radical way with a previous repressive era. Rather, it is part of a longer and continuous history of which the apparently repressive Victorian era is but a part, and is first laid down in the confessional: 'The Christian pastoral prescribed as a fundamental duty the task of passing everything having to do with sex through the endless mill of speech.'[13]

It was not just the sexual act itself that was so rigorously controlled and monitored; increasingly, it was desire and thoughts. 'Examine diligently, therefore, all the faculties of your soul: memory, understanding, and will . . . Examine even unto your dreams, to know if, once awakened, you did not give them your consent,'[14] advised the Jesuit Paolo Segneri in the seventeenth century.

Attempting to hunt out the sexual in desires, thoughts and dreams, however, was inherently self-defeating. Like the comically impossible imperative, 'Do not think of a yellow elephant', the very exhortation to ban the sexual from the mind was an invitation to entertain it. As was recognized by Segneri, 'This matter is similar to pitch, for, however one might handle it, even to cast it far from oneself, it sticks none the less, and always soils.'[15] In trying to root out the sexual from every corner of the world and every recess of the mind, the world was sexualized as the mind was polluted. Attempts at censoring what could be thought and what could be seen compromised the censor into thinking what should not be thought and seeing what should not be seen. This was to remain the occupational hazard of the anti-pornographer right up to the twentieth century. (When Lord Longford made his investigation into pornography in the early 1970s, the cartoonists mercilessly lampooned him as investigator-cum-consumer of porn.) Censorship threatens to create what it seeks to control. The apparent opposition of the pornographic and the anti-pornographic weaves a web of illusion, as they are but two sides of the same coin.

△ German fifteenth-century woodcut, 'Thou shalt not commit adultery', the Sixth Commandment, from *Comfort for the Soul*, c.1480. Sexual temptation was the Devil's work: demons were thought ready to encourage people to stray sexually.

In the Middle Ages, sex became demonized. Unwelcome thoughts of sex by celibate clergy were often blamed on the Devil. Some monks blamed the Devil for ejaculations during sleep. One puzzling case that troubled the Church authorities concerned a young monk who kept ejaculating whenever he tried to pray. An evil spirit, reported Gerald of Wales (c. 1146– 1223), 'places its hands on his genital organs and does not stop rubbing his body with his own until he is so agitated that he is polluted by an emission of semen'. The solution was for the monk to fast and press a crucifix on 'those members over which the enemy dares (beyond belief) to triumph'.[16]

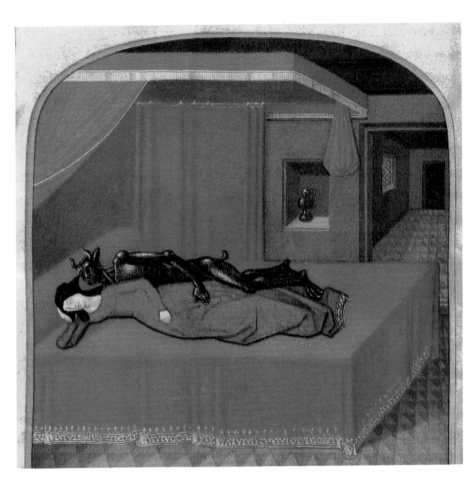

▷ Fourteenth-century illumination for the *Histoire de Merlin*.

It was a common belief that demons were ever eager to encourage inappropriate sexual encounters. And it was also believed – indeed, it was recognized in law – that they operated as incubi (demons that took the male form) and succubi (demons that took the female form) in order to have sexual intercourse with men and women as they slept.

The association of sex with the Devil eventually reached heady levels in the gathering hysteria over witches. These servants of the Devil were often thought to offer sex as part of their diabolical exchange. In brutal attempts to make reality conform with fantasy, the Church authorities succeeded in wringing a number of confessions from women sufficiently different to warrant an accusation of witchcraft. In Padua in 1265 a woman confessed that she had slept with a horned goat. In Kilkenny in 1324, Petronilla of Meath, after being flogged six times, confessed that she had witnessed a demon have intercourse with Lady Alice Kyteler, who had the misfortune of being rich and envied. Along with lurid and macabre tales of concoctions of dead men's nails and cocks, intestines being boiled in the skull of a decapitated robber, Lady Alice was accused of having sex with her own private demon.[17]

The fear of sexual demons was just part of a general identification of sex with the Devil that is apparent in woodcuts and drawings, like Francesco Parmigianino's *Witches'*

◁ *Witches' Sabbath* by
Parmigianino, 1530.

Sabbath (1530), where the Devil's servants clamber around a huge phallus. This is a long
way from the straightforward sexual imagery of Pompeii, and the demonization of sex
under Christianity reached its logical conclusion when the libidinous satyr of antiquity,
with its horns, pointed ears, tail and cloven hoofs, once again featured in popular
iconography, this time as the Devil.

In an era when sex was marginalized, it is perhaps inevitable that depictions of sex
and the body manifest the deep ambivalence of the age. Nor is it surprising, since the
Church was the principal patron of artistic production, that representations of sex are
relatively rare throughout the early Christian and medieval periods. As the twelfth-
century monk Peter of Celle warned, invoking Deuteronomy 5:8, 'The Law prohibited

not just the reality of these things [the desires of the flesh] but even their likeness.'[18]

While casting a shadow of shame and transgression, danger and ungodliness on to the representation of sex to the present day, however, the Church did not obliterate the sexual image altogether. Within this profoundly negative view of sex, when they did appear, images of the naked body or images of sex served as visual reminders of the fallen state of mankind. And while the grip of the Augustinian interpretation held good, the image of the naked female in particular would be not so much erotic as admonitory.

△ Sheela-na-gig carved on the exterior of Kilpeck Church, Hereford & Worcestor.

This is nowhere more in evidence than with the astonishing carvings found in Britain and Ireland, known as sheela-na-gigs (and also as 'Julia the Giddy, or the Girl of the Paps, or the Whore, or the Idol, or Cathleen Owen, or Sheila Dwyer...'[19]). These remarkable hymns to sexual repulsion have ugly large heads, bulbous eyes, open mouths and disproportionate gaping vulvas. Sometimes the women hold open their giant labia in a pantomime display of sexual invitation. These remarkable images were to be found in even more remarkable places: the doors and walls of medieval churches. They leered at the parishioners of Kilpeck, Hereford & Worcester, taunted the godly of Cavan in Ireland, and exposed themselves to the devout of Easthorpe in Essex.

The history of these loose and wanton 'sheelas' remains fogged by acts of censorship. From the records, we can conclude that many more once existed than survive today. In 1631 the provincial statutes for Tuam, County Galway, required parish priests to hide away and keep hidden these 'fat figures of unpleasant features' and in 1676 Bishop Brehan in Waterford ordered that sheela-na-gigs were to be burned.[20] Our understanding has been further limited (with some recent significant exceptions[21]) by scant or maginalized scholarship. As a result, the provenance and significance of the sheelas is still uncertain, but whether they were remnants of pagan fertility cults, figures to ward off the evil eye or contemporary commissions, in the context of Church teaching about sex they would surely have been read as sermons in stone against lust and fornication.[22]

It was not only whorish old-hag exhibitionists that reinforced the official line. The Church could also afford to display much more enticing representations of women on its walls. With such unambiguously negative teachings on sex, there was little scope for misinterpretation by the flock. A carving on the lintel at Bourges Cathedral dating from the mid-thirteenth century showing a woman pulling back her clothes with one hand and touching herself with the other is unambiguous, according to Michael Camille, Professor of Art History at the University of Chicago: 'Even though she's so beautiful, that very physicality, that very beauty in her body, damns her eternally.'[23] This is the Last Judgement and she is standing to Christ's left. She is one of the damned – damned in fact by her own fallen female sexuality. Neither available nor desirable, she is the path to Hell.

Woman spelled sex and sex spelled death. This was the message since the Fall. Eve,

◁ The Last Judgement.
Thirteenth-century
carvings on the lintel at
Bourges Cathedral in
France. (Bottom) This
woman stands at Christ's
left: she is damned by her
own fallen female
sexuality.

ever the symbol of temptation and doom, appears attractive in medieval art only to underline her treacherous nature. The equation of women, sex and death was an old idea that would outlast the Middle Ages and is graphically revealed in Hans Baldung's *Death and Maiden* (1517). Death – half skeletal, half withered flesh – scrabbles and scratches for purchase on the young woman's breast with one hand while clasping at her hair to twist her head back to meet a suffocating embrace by a face half rotted away. At the same time, the smooth, white, inviting flesh of the woman is on display, directly addressing the (presumed male) viewer as an invitation that can be accepted only at the price of identifying with Death. To view the painting means travelling the route to death, just as desire leads nowhere else.

The kind of fevered identification of sexuality with death has its roots in the mindset of the earliest Christians, as monks went to the desert alone to find God. When one monk took in a woman who was lost, he burned his fingers on a flame through the night

to remind himself of the tortures of damnation. Another, on finding out that a beautiful woman he had once loved had died, dipped his clothes into her decaying body and lived with the smell to remind himself of the mortality of beauty and the reality of death.[24]

It was the terrors of the Last Judgement that presented the Middle Ages with the ultimate warning of the wages of sexual sin. The damned were frequently represented being tortured on those parts of the body that had been the site of their sin. The abdomens of lustful women were sucked out by serpents who entered through the vagina – fitting punishment for those who had made the cardinal error of mistaking the phallus as a source of pleasure. *The Last Judgement* by Giotto in the Arena Chapel at Padua (c.1303–10) shows four miserable sinners: one man is being hung up by his tongue, one woman by her long tresses, and the other man and woman by their genitals. The body has become an instrument of pain, anguish and torment; their nakedness reveals a sexuality that has been their undoing. These four sinners are surrounded by the damned being tormented by demons. Unlike many medieval images of naked men, whose genitals are in as insignificant a state as the rest of the body, here the genitals are large, announcing the cause of their perdition.

△ Detail of four sinners from *The Last Judgement* by Giotto (1267–1337), at the Arena Chapel, Padua.

◁ *Death and the Maiden* (1517) by Hans Baldung.

And again, on the carvings of Bourges Cathedral, while the saved are depicted clothed or with small, infantalized genitals, the damned have their sexuality emphasized. The demons are hairy, with huge penises. Toads cling to women's breasts. Demons sprout faces from various orifices; one in particular, stoking the fires of Hell with a pair of bellows, far to the left of Christ, has an ugly grinning anus. As Michael Camille says, 'The very organs that we might think of as organs of pleasure and sexuality, the orifices – the vagina, the arse, the mouth – in this Hell they're all turned into hideous screaming or grinning mouths. Hell is an orifice of the human body.' And Bourges was not alone. Many cathedrals in Europe had similarly robust imagery, although much of it was subsequently effaced by whitewashing and selective iconoclasm.

Michael Camille, who has made a number of pioneering studies of the images at the edges of medieval texts, cathedrals, churches and monasteries, says:

As well as being bibles in stone for the illiterate, these great Gothic cathedrals are also very much controlling mechanisms. Controlling people's views of sexuality. For us Hell is a fiction, but for people in the Middle Ages it was a possibility they were constantly reminded of. People believed that the end of time could come any day. It could be in twenty years, it could be in five minutes. They saw it as a temporal event, as something that would happen. These then are not erotic images in our sense of the word. They might have aroused for a moment but their whole point was to arouse in order to deny sexual feeling or pleasure.[25]

△ (Top) A prince and three girls in carvings from the temples at Khajuraho, built between 950 and 1050. Positive images of sexuality on Indian temples contrast with the more negative imagery on medieval temples in Europe. (Bottom) Japanese print of lovers by a landscape screen, *c.*1768, by Haranobu. Manuals of sexual knowledge, 'pillow books', were common in Japan.

The singular nature of this religiously framed negativity is thrown into sharp relief by the temples at Khajuraho in India, which were built between the tenth and eleventh centuries at roughly the same time as the European cathedrals. Here the sexual poses and acts are carved in graphic and celebratory abandon. Like the Hindu literature that describes the sexual activities of the gods and details various sexual positions, these carvings were a long way from warnings against sex and sin. There is the rhythm of life here, a celebration of the union of male and female, and of existence in all its forms. For the West, these temples serve as reminders of other possible worlds.

So embedded is the association of sex with sin in our collective consciousness, so deeply woven is the ambivalence towards sex and sexual representation, that we do not always see its peculiarity.

Not that all images of the naked body and of sex in the Christian West served the didactic purpose of the Church. Indeed, some were so irreverently secular that they seem to undo it. Just as sex was marginalized in society as a whole, these particular images are to be found in the margins of texts, at the edges of richly illuminated manuscripts of the thirteenth, fourteenth and fifteenth centuries. Very often – and remarkably to eyes that are unused to seeing the religious and the profane together – these irreverent marginal images appear in prayer books, like the Books of Hours.

At that time, few people possessed manuscripts or books. If a family owned any such thing it would probably be a Book of Hours, the devotional work used to take one through the prayers and thoughts for the day. Often beautifully and lavishly illustrated with images of the Virgin, the Annunciation and the Nativity, they could also be crammed with a profusion of chaotic marginalia – gambolling apes and jugglers, and any number of scenes that seem quite at odds with the central religious theme. It appears that whatever was interesting to people found expression in these books, even if that meant juxtaposing the religious and the profane. In fact, such combinations are so common that 'religious' and 'profane' are inadequate categories with which to understand the books and the age that produced them.

The sex in these and other medieval texts was often coded, but in ways that were

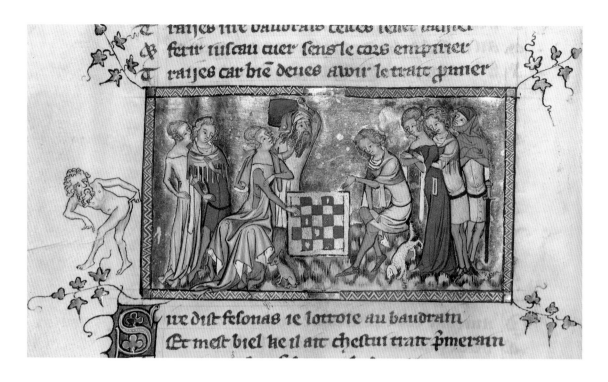

transparent to their readers. Looking at them today, we have to learn how to crack these codes, the meanings of which have been lost over the centuries. This is another example of the slow process of piecing together lost histories of the sexual image, for despite the fact that these particular examples have been crowding the margins of manuscripts for well over half a millennium, up until very recently they have been all but ignored.

As Roger Wieck, the curator of Medieval and Renaissance Manuscripts at the Pierpont Morgan Library in New York, explains, 'I've been fortunate as a curator to have access to hundreds of manuscripts, so that I can go through them, and its only such exposure that has begun to reveal to me the extent of the kind of erotic business that's going on in the margins. There is a code to be cracked. You might see a particular picture – let's say of a man with a very tall hat – and you might think, well, that's completely innocent. But if you go through a book with erotic marginalia on every page, or every other page, as you begin to go through it you can crack the code, because actually you're learning the language as you go, so that tall hats begin to suggest something else.'[26]

Tall hats, it seems, suggest sexual excitement. One illustration from a secular manuscript, the fourteenth-century *Les Voeux du Paon*, shows a penitent who has been beating his back with a whip which is down by his knee. Wearing a *very* tall hat, he is kneeling to kiss the naked buttocks of a monk. The whip itself has little strings coming out of the end of the cord, a reference to his own erect and ejaculating penis. Another image plays with the same idea. The penitent with a bloody back who has been flagellating himself now

△▽ (Top) A man displays his buttocks to chess players. Imagery in the margins of medieval texts, (*Les Voeux du Paon* pictured here, *c.*1340) are often irreverant commentaries on the central text. (Bottom) An image on the edge of a medieval Book of Hours, *c.*1320s: a bird pushes its long beak into a naked couple.

holds the whip erect, with cords shooting out in front of him – a reference again to masochistic pleasure. Once you've broken the code, apparently innocent figures acquire a new meaning. For example, an older man wrestling with a younger one in a seemingly mundane fashion turns into an image of homosexuality.

Depictions of sex itself are rare, and depictions of homosexual sex are rarer still. However, in one gloriously luxurious thirteenth-century Psalter – another form of devotional book – there is a clear if minuscule depiction of homosexual sex to the side of the text which can be seen with the help of a magnifying glass.

That these images play about in the margins provides a fitting symbolism. The texts reflect medieval ideas of the natural order of the world, with God at the centre and man, in his fallen state, at the outer edges. The clusters of playful jugglers, gambolling apes and defecating humans that populate the edges of these manuscripts, along with the coded references to sex, are but aspects of man's chaotic state in relation to God. Rather than being challenges or threats to the central message of the Church, the meaningless and abject forms are symbols of God's punishment after the Fall.

While mischievous, these are not radical rebellions against Christian authority. According to Michael Camille, they can be seen as jokes, and, like jokes, they ultimately leave everything as it is. Sometimes the joke can shock even modern sensibilities. One mid-fifteenth-century Book of Hours from Italy shows the First Bath of Christ. The Virgin is holding the Christ child, helped by two handmaidens, and they're filling the tub and testing the water. Yet in the middle of this rather ordinary scene is a remarkable detail: the child has an apparently huge penis. On closer inspection, this turns out to be the fingers of the Virgin poking between his legs! It is a sexual joke on the part of the artist. According to Roger Wieck, who is familiar with these visual puns on the genitals of Jesus, the joke shows us something about attitudes then and now: 'From our standpoint it's completely audacious, because the artist is using the figure of the Christ child itself to make these jokes. And it's at that moment when you realize the humour that can be made literally on the body of Christ means that the definition of sexual humour is just totally different from what we have today. If a modern artist did this today, I can't imagine what would happen to him. It couldn't be done today.'[27]

*

The legacy of the Church goes further than associating sex with sin; it goes further than casting a shadow of shame on the erotic image and hemming it in with guilt and fear. Christianity cast its own peculiar brand of erotics over images of the naked body. Sado-masochism and eroticized depictions of suffering, for instance, have a long tradition in Western art and the tradition has its roots in the history of the Church. The third and early fouth centuries, when Christianity was still a minority religion in the Roman Empire, witnessed a wave of persecutions and horrific martyrdoms of early Christians. This scratched a scar

△ (Top) A penitent kissing the buttocks of a monk, from the secular manuscript *Les Voeux du Paon*, 1340. (Bottom) Mid-thirteenth-century Psalter, showing a naked male couple.

▷ The First Bath of the Christ Child', in a Book of Hours from Italy dated 1470. Medieval visual puns on the genitals of Jesus may be surprising to modern eyes.

Eus Ad primam.
in adiutorium me
um intente. Do
mine adadiuuan

△ *St Sebastian*, c.1480, by Andrea Mantegna. The depiction of the martyrdom of the saints was eroticized in the hands of Renaissance artists.

on the mindset of the religion that is visible in its art through the centuries. In addition to the central image of the Passion, the suffering Christ on the Cross, the final trials of the saints presented artists with a unique combination of religious devotion and physical pain for their palettes. Add to this the naked body, the depiction of which became conventional in religious tableaux (like the Fall, the Passion and the Last Judgement) and you have a heady combination of devotional passion, physical agony and nudity.

Savage methods of torture that had been banned throughout the Mediterranean were used against the Christians. Eusebius, Bishop of Caesarea (260–339), recounts the fates of those who refused to renounce their faith under Diocletian (245–313). Of the martyrs in Pontus, for example:

> Sharp reeds were driven through their fingers under the tips of the nails; in the case of others, lead was melted down by fire, and the boiling, burning stuff poured down their backs, roasting the most essential parts of their body; others endured in their privy parts and bowels sufferings that were disgraceful, pitiless, unmentionable, which the noble and law-abiding judges devised with more than usual eagerness displaying their cruelty as if it were some great stroke of wisdom; striving to outdo one another by ever inventing novel tortures, as if contending for prizes in a contest.[28]

After a thousand years of Christian culture in which martyrdom played a central role, artists developed a spectacular vocabulary based on the erotic aspects of suffering. Sebastian (d. c.288) was a particularly popular subject. According to legend, he was a Christian who served in Diocletian's praetorian guard. On hearing that he favoured Christians, the emperor ordered him to be shot by Mauretian archers, but they failed to kill him. Left for dead, he was nursed back to health by a woman named Irene, only to be beaten to death at a later time. At first, and unpromisingly, Sebastian was depicted as an old Roman soldier, but over time he turned into a young man with fine and beautiful limbs, often barely clothed, thoroughly (and suggestively) pierced with arrows.

Throughout the fifteenth and sixteenth centuries, the combination of fervour, pain and nudity proved ever more intoxicating as the body became more voluptuous and sexual in the hands of Renaissance artists. One example is Sebastiano del Piombo's *Martyrdom of St Agatha* (1520). Legend has it that Agatha was sent to a brothel run by Aphrodisia and her six daughters – a common punishment for unrepentant Christian women. When she refused to renounce her faith, she was stretched on the rack, a

△ *The Martyrdom of St
Agatha*, 1520, by
Sebastiano del Piombo.
Art historian Edward
Lucie-Smith has called this
'a piece of pornography in
church'.

torture that was often accompanied by the tearing of the sides with iron hooks and
burning with torches, and then, as she was still unrepentant, her breasts were crushed
and cut off. According to legend, she was then sent to prison and was healed and
comforted by St Peter in a vision. Four days later she was rolled over hot coals mixed
with broken potsherds, when she died. As with St Sebastian's final beating, however, it
was not St Agatha's final agony on hot coals that inspired the artists; it was the more
promising disfigurement of her breasts.

Art historian, Edward Lucie-Smith says of Sebastiano del Piombo's *Martyrdom of St
Agatha*, 'This is really a piece of pornography in church. It's a piece of sado-masochism.
And how one regards a culture which produces this kind of thing and thinks it's perfectly
all right is frankly a difficult question. She is the Venetian type. She has big breasts,
swelling belly – she couldn't be more directly female. There is something odd on the
expression of the face. She looks almost with a sense of complicity at her executioner. It's
as if they are engaged in something together, a sick collaboration, which is part of the
sado-masochistic atmosphere of this picture.'

By the Renaissance, depictions of the human body were becoming more 'realistic'.
Picking up the classical baton that had been dropped for more than a millennium,
painters turned to a more man-centred, naturalistic mode of representation. According
to Giorgio Vasari (1511–74), who wrote on the history of the arts in Italy from the
thirteenth to the sixteenth centuries, as well as being an artist and architect himself, 'Art

△ *St Sebastian with the Angel,* a painting after Fra Bartolomeo (a contemporary copy of the original of 1514). The original painting is said to have so aroused women in church that it had to be removed.

rose from humble beginnings to the summit of perfection': the goal was the mastery of representation, as each artist built on another's skill in perspective, colour and shading. The ideal, it seems, was to create an illusion of lifelikeness; the power of painting was to deceive the eye.

Such mastery of representation however, had an unsettling effect when applied to the naked body. Vasari recounts how Fra Bartolomeo (*c.*1474–1517) painted a beautiful St Sebastian that had to be removed from its church in Florence when women revealed during confession that they had sinned while looking at it. Vasari notes that the painting has this effect because of the skill of Bartolomeo. This power of the more realistic paintings to arouse sexually has tended to be ignored or denied as the paintings have been assimilated into the high-art canon, and yet this was not the case at the time. Vasari tells the story of the Florentine who asked Toto de Nunziato, the puppet painter, for a Madonna that would not be an incitement to desire; he obliged by painting a Madonna with beard.[29] Thanks to the mimetic skills of the Renaissance painters, the saints were becoming objects of desire.

This trend was not welcome in all quarters. The increasingly voluptuous imagery that was being produced was straining the patience of the Church. It was one thing to have images that reinforced the Church's teachings; it was quite another to have images that undermined them. In the backlash that accompanied the Counter-Reformation in the latter part of the sixteenth century, overly salacious imagery was targeted. Reforming archbishops like Gabriele Paleotti in Bologna and Federico Borromeo in Milan examined the content of paintings and sculptures. In 1586 Paleotti wrote, 'For that which concerns obscenities painted in a lascivious and provocative manner, or showing unseemly limbs, one should impede even their private possession. In the future, whoever dares to paint and sculpt them will be severely punished as a corrupter of manners.'[30]

The Last Judgement (1536–41), Michelangelo's Sistine Chapel fresco of the saved rising from their graves to heaven and the damned being dragged down to Hell, was considered by many at the time as obscene. When the papal master of ceremonies, Biagio da Cesena, first saw it, he ventured the opinion that 'it was a very improper thing to paint so many nude forms, all showing their nakedness in that shameless fashion, in so highly honoured a place', thinking that 'such pictures were better suited to a bathroom, or a road-side wine shop, than to a chapel of a Pope'. This plain speaking earned him immortality of a kind when he was promptly painted into Hell by an irritated Michelangelo. The story goes that the enraged Biagio immediately demanded that his image be removed, but evidently without success, since his leering presence with ass's ears and a huge serpent twisted around his body and biting at his genitals is still visible today. Not even an appeal to the Pope, Paul III, succeeded: he is supposed to have replied 'Messer Biagio, you know that I have authority in heaven and on earth, but this authority does not extend into Hell. You will be patient if I cannot liberate you from there.'[31]

More scandalized voices were to be heard when the fresco was revealed to the public in October 1541, prompting admiration and outrage in equal portion. As the poet Pietro Aretino (1492–1557) wrote to Michelangelo in 1545, 'Michelangelo, whom all admire, has chosen to display to the whole world an impiety of irreligion only equalled by the perfection of his painting.'[32] The Council of Trent issued a decree in 1564 that the offending parts of the fresco should be covered up. Michelangelo was lucky –

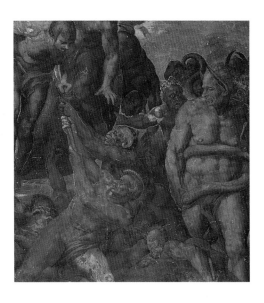

△ Detail from *The Last Judgement* by Michelangelo (1475–1564). The artist painted Biagio da Cesena, the papal secretary, into his masterpiece – in Hell.

some were demanding its complete destruction, as indeed was the fate of a number of overly explicit images during the Counter-Reformation. None the less, when Michelangelo learned that the Pope wanted him to change the painting, he is said to have replied, 'The Pope has merely to change the world and I will paint the new one.'[33]

Fighting talk, however, did not prevent the great cover-up. Wisps of fabric and loincloths were painstakingly painted over the male genitalia. In fact, the appropriate volume and density of loincloth were evidently subject to great scrutiny, as alteration after alteration was made over the years. They continued to at least the eighteenth century, and close examination reveals that the loincloth covering St Peter was an amendment to a previous smaller loincloth underneath.[34] St Catherine was originally naked; in the changes made to cover up the 'obscenities', she acquired a voluminous green garment. Even more telling was the fate of St Blaise, whose position behind St Catherine was seen as unacceptably sexual. The solution was to alter the position of his head, so that instead of leaning over St Catherine his face was turned towards Christ – a major revision that was to the detriment of the naturalness of the original composition.

The ironic if inevitable result of the systematic covering-up of *The Last Judgement* was that engravings and copies of the original – in all its glorious nudity – became highly valued. The original version became the naughty version, which in turn became an object of desire. It is an example of the way in which the very act of censorship creates what it seeks to control; the way in which censorship creates not only objects of (newly) illicit desire but also markets to go with them.

We are back to the original preoccupations of the Church. Sex was not supposed to be something flaunted but rather something to be hidden away, and if it was portrayed at all the portrayal was expected to reveal its abjection, its misery, its lack of glory. The naked body was to be seen as humble. The naked body, when represented, was to emphasize man's natural state in relation to God.

And yet here, during the Renaissance, gathering pace, was nudity as an erotic display. It was as if the Church was losing control over the way nudity would be read. No longer

▷ (Overleaf left) A contemporary copy by Marcello Venusti (*c.*1512–1579) of Michelangelo's *The Last Judgement* in the Sistine Chapel. From contemporary copies we can see the composition of the original *Last Judgement* in all its nudity. (Overleaf right) *The Last Judgement* by Michelangelo. Much of the original nudity was covered up with painted loin cloths as a result of the Counter-Reformation.

▷ Details from *The Last Judgement* by Michelangelo. (Top, left and right) St Bartholomew before and after the cover-up. (Bottom, left and right) St Catherine and St Blaise before and after the cover-up.

was it certain that the paintings on church walls and the carvings outside cathedrals would be read as sermons, that the erotic potential in religious images would be raised only to be extinguished again in visions of the Last Judgement. The balance had shifted and it seemed that the erotic now threatened to undermine the sacred.

If religious subjects sometimes offered a thinly veiled excuse for nudity, when it came to subjects from classical mythology the veil could be as transparent as a name: Venus. It seemed as if it was enough to slap a classical name on to a picture of a naked woman to clothes her with respectability, a logic that is even more firmly entrenched today. From a modern viewpoint, these paintings can be difficult to see as anything other than emblems of high art and the embodiment of culture (they are in museums after all, grown-up places – worthy, solid, decent, respectable places). They are *high* art and therefore we must look *up* to them; they have stature. The works have become part of the canon and therefore are unquestioned conveyors of suitable culture. And yet this does not mean that they were unquestioned at the time (or indeed unquestionable today). As Edward Lucie-Smith says, 'I think the more that one looks at the history of art,

the more one finds that it is involved with the idea of the transgressive and the outrageous. Renaissance Venuses are very much connected with this idea of transgression, and this had been smoothed over by our society by putting them in museums and saying yes, yes, they're wonderful. Yet they're not saying easy things at all. They're saying rather sharply erotic things. I think that we have a curious kind of consensus in our society to ignore the pornographic content of images which are considered to be classics.'[35]

△ *Venus of Urbino* (1538) by Titian. Mark Twain called the classic painting the 'obscenest picture the world possesses'.

This return to the classical ideal of the 'convincing' or 'realistic' image in the Renaissance brought with it greater capacity for arousing desire. If Titians were once kept in the bedchamber to promote lustful thoughts, this association has been broken by the placing of Titians in public galleries. But the arousing nature of the paintings was obvious at the time they were produced, and later too, to those willing to cut through the thicket of received wisdom about 'high art'. In the nineteenth century, Mark Twain said of the *Venus* of Urbino (1538):

You enter [the Uffizi] and proceed to that most-visited little gallery that exists in the world – the Tribune – and there, against the wall, without obstructing rag or leaf, you may look your fill upon the foulest, the vilest, the obscenest picture the world possesses – Titian's *Venus*. I saw a young girl stealing furtive glances at her; I saw young men gazing long and absorbedly at her; I saw aged infirm men hang upon her charms with a pathetic interest . . . Without any question it was

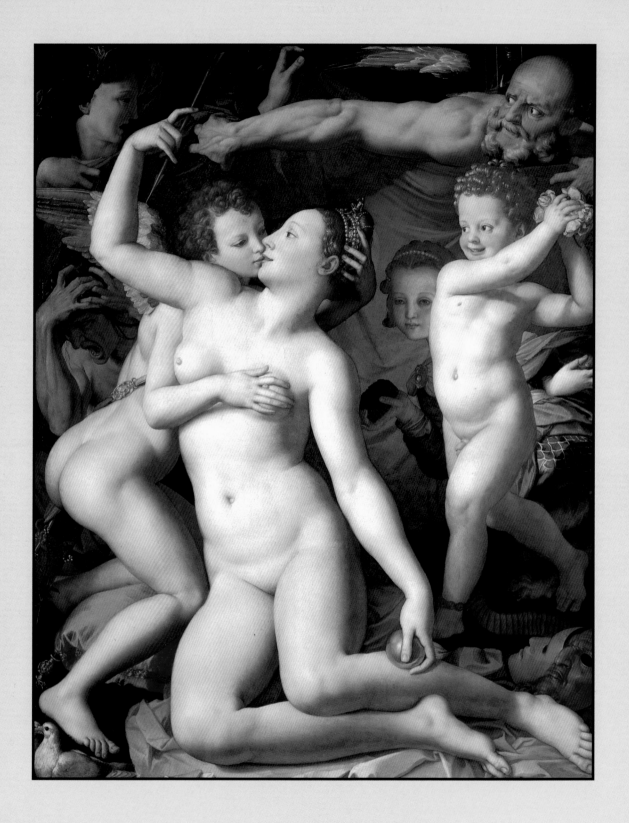

△ *Venus and the Organ Player* (c.1550) by Titian.

◁ *Venus, Cupid, Folly and Time* (1540–50) by Agnolo Bronzino. The canonical status of high art can sometimes blind us to its transgressive elements: this Bronzino touches on themes of paedophilia and incest.

painted for a bagnio and it was probably refused because it was a trifle too strong. In truth it is a trifle too strong for any place but a public art gallery.[36]

The power of an image to arouse is seen as more relevant to pornography than to art, which is motive enough to ignore its presence in high art. Art and pornography are seen as mutually exclusive, at opposite ends of the spectrum: one is high, contemplative and transcendent; one is low, designed to arouse, and base.

Art historian Edward Lucie-Smith dismisses those who prefer to ignore the pornographic elements of high art which can even embrace the taboos of paedophilia and incest. Of Bronzino's *Venus, Cupid, Folly and Time* he says, 'I sometimes wonder what those people who lead school parties around the National Gallery actually have to say about this picture. What do they tell the kids? It's deliberately transgressive. Here you have a female nude, Venus, who is about to be French-kissed by an adolescent who is in fact her son. And Cupid's bottom is stuck out in a most provocative way: it's almost as if he's offering himself for a sexual act.'[37]

Concerns over the more comely bodies in Renaissance art went further than fears about the ungodly portrayal of the naked body. They indicated the levels of anxiety about the power of the sexual, the result of over one thousand years of the denigration and disparagement of sex. Banned to the margins, sex had acquired power – the power of subversion. The rules that confined sex and sexual images were vulnerable to disobedience. Rules can be broken, and the people who break them are engaged in a

▷ (Left) The statue of Michelangelo's *David* (1501–1504) with figleaf. (Right) David without figleaf: to Michelangelo's disgust the figleaf was added in the sixteenth century. It was not removed until the twentieth century.

subversive act. People who break rules and get away with it are exercising power.

It is no coincidence that the Reformation, which gave secular rulers an opportunity to acquire power independent from Rome, coincided with the proliferation of such images. Take *Venus and the Organ Player* (1548) by Titian. Venus, completely exposed to the viewer, with her hair done up like a Venetian prostitute, is lying stark naked while a fully dressed man at a set of phallic organ pipes is staring directly and unmistakably at her genitals. As Edward Lucie-Smith says of the painting, which was commissioned by Philip II of Spain, arch-enemy of the protestants, 'It's a really very odd picture in a way for such a personage to commission, because it's extremely erotic. It could hardly be a more directly sexy picture. And I think the thing we have to ask ourselves is how such a picture came to be commissioned by such a person. On Titian's side we know that he was a dirty old man. But Philip II – that's rather different, isn't it? The King is making a statement about his position by commissioning a picture of this kind. He is saying, "I don't have to obey the ordinary rules. What is not allowed to you is allowed to me." That is what the picture is about.'[38]

For the moment, however, the subversive power of the sexual image was still largely contained. In a world where the Church played such a central role in the production and display and destruction of texts and images (at least for the vast majority of the population), the sexual image was controlled. And in the instances when a wealthy patron was in a position to commission more unbuttoned images, the circle of privileged viewers was rendered harmless not only by limited numbers but also by social position.

This would ultimately change with the impact of the invention of print, when the subversive power invested by the Church in the sexual image would be used effectively

△ *Birth of Venus* (c.1485)
by Sandro Botticelli.

◁ *Birth of Venus* from the
House of Venus, Pompeii.
(*c.* first century). It took
fourteen hundred years,
the Christian reworking of
the story of the Fall, and
the problematization of
sex to change the
straightforwardness of
Pompeii's naked Venus into
an aesthetic of sexual
shame in Botticelli's self-
conscious Venus. [39]

against both the Church and the State, and would no longer be so containable. For not only would printed pornography* be harder to destroy by single acts of censorship but it would also reach a wider audience with less invested in the prevailing social order.

---

* Inevitably, we see history backwards, and the concepts created by historical processes are the only ones we have to understand history itself. Even though 'pornography' is an invention of the nineteenth century, we now live in a 'post-pornographic' world, and see things with 'post-pornographic' eyes. Rather than substitute forced and unnatural terms, I shall continue to use terms like 'pornographic' in pre-nineteenth-century contexts, where it seems appropriate in talking of the sexually transgressive and censored image.

The Devil's Press

I n a striking and memorable catch phrase, the writer Marshall McLuhan asserted in the 1960s that 'the medium is the message'.[1] For McLuhan, the content of any individual piece of work was less relevant to human action, to social reality and to actual experience than the medium in which it appeared, because it was the medium that determined who got to see it and how it was seen. By extending our reach we extend ourselves. The idea that a new technology changes our perceptual horizons, reconfiguring our ways of seeing, is as applicable to the history of pornography as it is to anything else. Different technologies – whether paint, print, photography, film, video or digital – make different demands on our senses, foregrounding the one, eclipsing the other, realigning them to give a brand-new perception of the world.

The invention of print altered the traditional lines of the transmission of knowledge while simultaneously rupturing the traditional lines of social control. Individuals were no longer tied to images publicly displayed and officially sanctioned by the Church, no longer tied to the similarly sanctioned manuscripts that were in a foreign language (Latin), and no longer so tied to the oral transmission of texts through authority figures (priests). The printed word and the printed image opened the door to a new world of revolutionary, transgressive, and ultimately pornographic, possibilities.

The new technology brought trouble almost from the start. On 31 October 1517 an obscure German monk pinned his ninety-five theses to the door of the church at Wittenberg, attacking the Church's practice of selling indulgences. It was an unremarkable start to what would be a turning point in the history of Europe. As in Chaos theory, where the flap of butterfly wings on one continent will end up causing hurricanes on another, the nailing of a small protest to a church door ended up shaking the Church to its foundations. Martin Luther's ninety-five theses were in Latin and incomprehensible to the majority of people at the time. As the seemingly baffled Augustinian theologian would explain – perhaps a little disingenuously – six months later to the Pope, 'They were meant exclusively for our academic circle here.'[2] Instead,

◁ Count de Waldeck drawing (1858) reproduces one of the notorious *Postures*, based on a number of different sexual positions, first engraved by Marc'Antonio Raimondi in the sixteenth century.

[73]

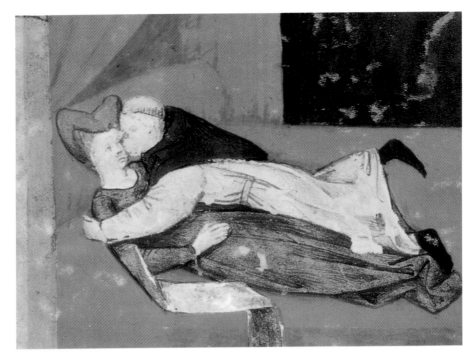

▷ A monk and nun on a bed in a fourteenth-century illumination from Boccaccio's *Decameron*. Boccaccio sought to tell 'life as it is' in his *Decameron*, which included the sexual exploits of the supposedly celibate clergy. Many of the early manuscripts were richly illustrated.

translated and printed, they were known throughout Germany in a fortnight and Europe in a month.

Johannes Gutenberg is credited with the invention of the printing process in the mid-fifteenth century. It was the invention of print that turned the forum for debate from the village square to the cities of Europe, and it was the invention of print that pushed obscure lives – still blinking – into the limelight of history. Between 1517 and 1520 Luther produced some thirty publications and these probably sold well over 300,000 copies.[3] Print unleashed a new age of communication, connecting people who might have nothing more in common than shared dissatisfaction. It provided direct communication between unorthodox thinkers and a wider audience. Tracts were passed around and pamphlets with titles like 'The Pope Donkey' were printed, with caricatures ridiculing the 'Antichrist Pope' and the Church of Rome.[4] It was a spiral of dissent: the more publications there were in circulation, the more widespread the heretical beliefs, the more publications were in demand, the more were produced. There were extensive underground networks, connected by hawkers and willing booksellers who, if they did not risk open display, would secrete the books and pamphlets in cellars and storerooms.[5]

This was dangerous stuff and the authorities were quick to recognize it, if uneven and inconsistent in their attempts to deal with the problem. Once welcomed by the Church as 'a peaceful art' (producing, as it did, early religious works such as the famous Gutenberg Bible of 1452), the printing press had turned into an instrument of subversion and action was taken. In some cases, measures were draconian. Books and booksellers were ordered to be burned, like the printer and the bookseller in France who were burned in November 1534 for having printed and bound the 'false works' of Luther.

In fact, at one point, all printing of books was banned by decree in France in 1535 on pain of death by hanging.[6] Soon whole bodies of legislation were developing to put a stop to the production and sale of forbidden books, the steady expansion of which testified to the steady increase in heretical beliefs. Suppression, however, was a rearguard action that was ultimately ineffective; the genie was out of the bottle and nothing would induce it to go back in.

The print medium is so ubiquitous today that we are liable to take its genius for granted. The original process was simple, requiring not much more than movable metal type, a fatty-based ink and a press. Its very simplicity, however, had profound implications. The essential power of print was its ability to create copies: to reproduce mechanically a single text in *quantity*. And the ability to reproduce a single text in quantity made that text relatively inexpensive. This fact, together with their portability, meant that books and pamphlets could be distributed and then carried away and, if necessary, hidden. The printed book also brought with it a market. As Marshall McLuhan has said, print was the first mass-produced commodity, subject to rudimentary laws of supply and demand. Commerce had entered into the equation. Whether there was a market was determined by what people wanted, which was not quite the same as what the authorities might want. While the rich had always been able to access illustrated, and sometimes titillating, manuscripts or paintings, such practices were no longer their exclusive preserve but were extended to the literate middle classes – the lawyers, lay advisers at court, merchants, town citizens and even women. Print was ultimately a great leveller.

If print was the thorn in its side, sex was the Achilles' heel of the Church. The high standards of chastity set by the early Church fathers proved impossible to meet. By the time of the Reformation, some convents had become almost brothels, according to one of the papal private secretaries.[7] The original ascetic project of the early Christians created a rod for the Church's back. Sex endangered not only the souls of individual Christians but also the authority of the Church itself. The clergy were pilloried for failure to live up to their own sexual teachings, and allegations of hypocrisy fuelled the Reformation. This was uncomfortable territory made more so by the arrival of the printing press. From now on the sexual exploits – real and imagined – of the clergy could be exploited mercilessly by sexually explicit imagery and ribald pamphlets and books.

△ Two people naked on a bed from Boccaccio's *Decameron*. Many early editions of the *Decameron* used wood engravings as illustrations.

One of the earliest examples of the dynamics of the combination of sex, print and repression can be seen in Boccaccio's *The Decameron*, which initially appeared in autograph manuscript form in Venice in 1371. This was, in the author's words, 'the representation of life as it is'. Set against the backdrop of the plague that ravished Florence in 1348, it tells of seven women and three men who escape to a sumptuous villa, where they entertain each other with stories, one each for the ten days they are there.

In the ninth story on the second day, an abbess in a Lombardy convent, Madonna Usimbalda, who is renowned for her piety, is told by a number of nuns in the middle of

the night that a young nun, Isabetta, has a male visitor in her cell. Unfortunately, at that moment the abbess has her own lover with her – a priest whom she frequently smuggles into her room in a chest. In her haste to get up, the abbess inadvertently puts the priest's breeches on her head with the braces dangling down at the sides, instead of her veil. Thus found out, she declares that it is impossible to withstand the assaults of the flesh and as long as discretion is maintained, all the nuns are at liberty to enjoy themselves. And those envious nuns who could find no lovers 'consoled themselves in secret as best they could'.[8]

The tenth story on the third day is 'How to Put the Devil in Hell'. It concerns a devout young hermit, Rustico, who takes a beautiful girl called Alibech into his cell when she asks him to teach her how to serve God. Failing in his fight against temptation, Rustico informs Alibech that the best way to serve God is to put the Devil back in Hell. When Alibech sees his erection – something the innocent girl has never seen before – Rustico informs her that this in fact is the Devil. When Alibech says that she is grateful not to have a Devil herself, he informs her that while she may not have a Devil she has Hell, 'At which point he conveyed the girl to one of their beds, where he instructed her in the art of incarcerating that accursed fiend.'[9]

In the 1420s *The Decameron* was subject to attack in sermons, and in 1497 it was burned in what would become known as the Bonfire of Vanities when Savonarola, the prior of San Marco in Florence and at the time the most powerful man in Florence, made a pyramid of wood nearly sixty feet high to which were added not only *The Decameron* but also 'immodest' foreign tapestries, musical instruments and works of art

△ French manuscript
illumination, *c.*1480, from
Boccaccio's *Decameron*.

– in fact anything that might distract people from God. During the Counter-Reformation
the anti-clericalism that had made *The Decameron* so delightful to Protestants meant it
was a prime target for inclusion on the Index of Prohibited Books, drawn up and made
official by the Council of Trent, and only the expurgated editions evaded censorship. In
the authorized editions, the monks became conjurors, the nuns aristocrats and the
Abbess Madonna Usimbalda a countess.

From the start, however, *The Decameron* had been a success. Early impassioned
readers and copyists spent hours personally transcribing the text. Manuscripts
circulated, some with exquisite illustrations, finding favour among the new merchant
classes. But it was only with the invention of print that it became a 'best-seller'. It was
one of the earliest printed books. By the end of the fifteenth century, there were more
than 8,000 illustrations of Boccaccio's texts in 300 different printed and manuscript
editions. Today, save for Dante's *Divine Comedy*, no work by an Italian has been
translated so often.

Attempts at suppression only consolidated the work's reputation, adding an aura of
illicit pleasure to its purchase that no doubt extended even to the expurgated editions. As
late as 1922, the postal authorities in Cincinnati seized copies and the bookseller involved
was fined $1,000. Five years later, US Customs mutilated a copy printed in England before

returning it. Under the Obscene Publications Act of 1857 in England copies have been destroyed on a number of occasions throughout the twentieth century by order of magistrates' courts.[10]

At about the same time as the printed word came the development of the printed image. The first woodcut that it is possible to date comes from the early fifteenth century, although printing from woodblocks is likely to have started in the late fourteenth century. Early prints were often devotional, showing saints and others thought to be able to cure illnesses or protect travellers. These were relatively inexpensive, easy ways for people to obtain images to carry round with them or keep at home, hanging them on walls or storing them in special places. The future, however, lay in engraving, which was increasingly used later in the fifteenth and in the early sixteenth centuries. The image was incised into a plate – usually copper – which was filled with ink and then paper was forced under pressure into the lines. Engraved plates lasted longer than woodblocks, as well as being better at showing detail, thus allowing a greater sophistication of image. Like the woodcuts, many were sold as souvenirs at pilgrimage sites or for personal devotional uses.

▽ *Venus and Mars at the Forge of Vulcan* (Second State) by Enea Vico after Parmigianino (1543). Engravings could be censored and plates scratched over: here the image of Venus and Mars in bed has been removed.

▷ Before and after: (top) *Venus and Mars at the Forge of Vulcan* (First State) by Enea Vico after Parmigianino (1543); (bottom) *Venus and Mars at the Forge of Vulcan* (Third State), after Venus had been put back on to the bed, alone.

The printed image proved no less revolutionary than the printed word. The image has a natural primacy over the word (as John Berger says, 'Seeing comes before words. The child looks and recognizes before it can speak,'[11]) and images inevitably had the potential to play a part in early polemics, being immediately accessible and intelligible. The printed image blurred the two previously distinct and clear-cut routes through which people encountered images: first, for the élite, there were privately owned decorated ornaments and paintings; then, for the vast mass of people, there were frescoes and paintings in public spaces like churches.[12] The development of print marked the beginning of a form of democratization of imagery as a whole, and that inevitably encompassed erotic imagery. In addition, features of the printed image – private ownership, portability and greater accessibility – would prove to be crucial in the development of particular pornographic forms (they have been essential to the twentieth-century phenomenon of the men's magazine, for instance). That privately held and portable images would be used as a vehicle for erotica had been foreshadowed in 1402 in the complaint made by Jean Gerson, Bishop of Paris, when he wrote of 'the filthy corruption of boys and adolescents by shameful and nude pictures offered for sale at the very temples and sacred places'.[13]

As is frequently shown by the history of pornography, the potential for wider accessibility prompted concern, which in turn prompted censorship. There was active censorship of sixteenth-century prints with erotic subjects, which were considered vulgar. As David Freedburg says, 'They can get into the hands of the *vulgus*, the crowd; they are therefore not like art, which is unique and in principle restricted in the access it offers to its audience.'[14] And so we have Zoan Andrea's *Couple Embracing* from the first half of the sixteenth century, where the man's hand that was originally down the front of the woman's dress was redrawn on top of the dress. Similarly Enea Vico's *Mars, Venus*

▷ 'Ovide et Corine'
(*c.*1602) by Agostino
Caracci from *Loves of the
Gods*. Caracci was a
prolific engraver of erotic
themes.

and Vulcan (1543), after Parmigianino, comes down to us in three different states: the first shows Mars and Venus on the bed in coitus, the second has the lovers removed, and the third shows Venus alone back on the bed and naked, but more modestly covered and asleep. The censorship may have taken place at the end of the sixteenth or the beginning of the seventeenth century, but such acts continued over the years. Prints of Agostino Carracci's *Lacivie* were altered, and Leo XIII destroyed hundreds of sixteenth-century plates, melting them down in the Tivoli foundry in 1823.[15] As David Freedburg says, 'The issue is at least as much social control as sexual control.'[16]

From the sixteenth century, then, sex and print proved to be a heady (and potentially subversive) combination. And nowhere were the pornographic possibilities of the new medium more clearly on display than in the story of the so-called *Aretine Postures*.

The story starts with Giulio Romano, the principle protégé of Raphael. Legend has it that in the early 1520s, furious that Pope Clement VII was delaying payment on some

commissioned work he was finishing after the death of Raphael, Romano drew scenes –
supposedly sixteen in all – of copulating couples on the walls of the Sala di Costantino
in the Vatican itself. Such an act, while no doubt bold and even reckless, has to be seen
in the context of a Vatican that mixed politics and religion, the secular and the sacred, the
affairs of God and the affairs of State on a scale soon to come under full-scale assault by
stubborn monks and stubborn kings in the Reformation. This was a world in which, for
example, at a banquet on All Saints' Eve in 1501 Pope Alexander VI is said to have
watched fifty naked courtesans crawling on all fours
to pick up chestnuts that were being thrown at
them.[17] And nor would Romano's paintings have been
the first erotic images on the walls of the Vatican. The
bathroom of Cardinal Bibbiena, above Raphael's
loggia on the third floor, was covered with erotic
pagan figures by Raphael and his students in 1515
after the apartments were damaged by fire. Rarely
acknowledged in the recent history of the Vatican, the
frescoes showed mythological scenes such as the
birth of Venus and Venus with Adonis. The subjects,
chosen by the Cardinal himself, were whitewashed
over in the nineteenth century and declared out of
bounds to visitors.

As for Giulio Romano's copulating couples,
exactly what these sixteen positions of sexual
intercourse looked like we do not know, since they
do not adorn the walls of the Sala di Costantino
today. In fact, not only is it unclear what the images
looked like; it is unclear whether they actually
adorned the Vatican walls at all. What we do know
is that they no longer exist.

The disappearance of the original paintings
epitomizes the fragility of the one-off original,
whether painting, fresco or drawing. The transgressive sexual image would always be vulnerable in

a censorious age. Due to this vulnerability, the phenomenon of pornography was limited
until the advent of mechanical reproduction. Once paid for by one person and created
by another, the original can easily be lost or destroyed by a third. Like Michelangelo's
painting of *Leda and the Swan*, which was commissioned by Duke Alfonso of Ferrara in
1529, and later formed part of the collections of King Francis I and King Louis XIII of
France. Unusually, this depicted the moment after the exertions of intercourse, with
the swan's neck lying between Leda's legs and its beak touching her lips as she lies back
exhausted. The image is reported to have been burned by one of Louis XIII's ministers as
a dangerous obscenity. And while we have some idea of what it was like from a
contemporary copy, the original has been lost for ever. The history of art is littered with
such examples: from the medieval illuminated manuscripts that have been handed down

△ (Top) *Leda and the Swan*
drawing, after
Michelangelo; (bottom)
Leda and the Swan
painting of 1868, after
Michelangelo.
Michelangelo's original
Leda and the Swan was
destroyed as an obscenity;
there are only copies left
in existence today.

△ *Giove Seduce Olimpiade*, by Giulio Romano (1492–1546), Palazzo Te, Mantua. The development of private patronage in the Renaissance allowed artists to be more transgressive – even by today's standards.

to us today in damaged or censored form – genitalia were vulnerable simply to being rubbed out by their disapproving readers, as was any kind of suggested sexual contact, even kissing lips; through the paintings destroyed and mutilated following the edicts of the Council of Trent as part of the Counter-Reformation clean-up; the frequent destruction of erotic collections on the death of the collector or artist, like John Ruskin's destruction of J.M.W. Turner's erotic drawings after his death in 1851 (although some of Turner's erotic output remains – for example, the drawing of a woman performing fellatio on a man and also a pen and ink close-up of a man's penis entering the vulva of a woman with her legs over his shoulders); the numerous paintings whose offending parts were painstakingly repainted by the Victorians; to examples of acts of dramatic protest, like Mary Richardson's slashing of the *Rokeby Venus* by Velázquez in the National Gallery, London, in 1914.

However 'pornographic' the content of the lost Giulio Romano's drawings, it was print that secured their notoriety. This again demonstrates the power of print, for it was

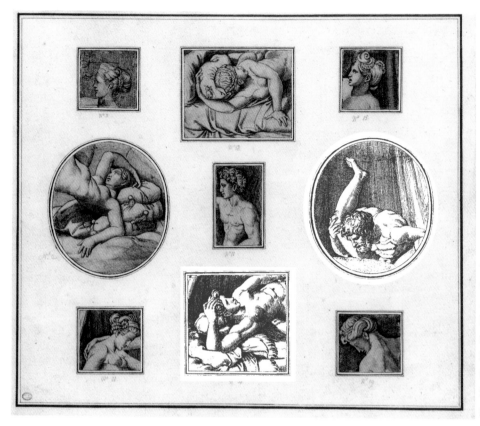

◁ Fragments of the
original engravings of the
Postures (c.1524) by
Marc'Antonio Raimondi,
now held at the British
Museum. The highlighted
fragments correspond to
the complete image on
page 84 (top).

not the original drawings themselves that caused the scandal surrounding the *Aretine Postures* but their publication. The story continued with Marc'Antonio Raimondi, the foremost engraver of the Italian Renaissance, who set about making engravings from the original drawings.

Raimondi's set of engravings appeared for sale in 1524 as the *Sedici Modi* or *Sixteen Positions*. They were an instant success and, according to Giorgio Vasari, were to be found 'in those places one would have least suspected' – presumably the papal court. There was an immediate furore and Cardinal Giberti, the papal censor, ordered the plates and all copies of the prints to be destroyed, and the death penalty for anyone who had the audacity to reprint them. Marc'Antonio Raimondi was thrown into jail. A similar fate might have befallen Giulio Romano himself, had he not had the good fortune to have as his patron at this time Duke Federico di Gonzaga of Mantua, where he found the freedom to paint the likes of his exceptional frescoes in the Room of Cupid and Psyche at the Palazzo Te, and where their explicitness was not considered a dangerous obscenity.

The unfortunate Marc'Antonio Raimondi was left to rot in jail, and was rescued only by the intervention of one Ippolito dei Medici, who became a cardinal soon after, and Baccio Bandinelli, without whose help, in the words of Vasari, he 'would have fared very badly'.[18]

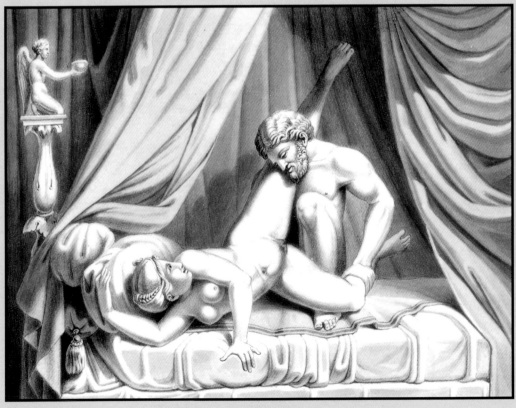

The attempt at censorship of the first set of engravings seems – unusually – to have been almost completely successful. Held in the vaults of the British Museum, one of the only original prints still in existence, itself a victim of censorship, is in bits. We have fragments of an arm here, a leg there, a head: enough to indicate vigorous sexual coupling, yet not enough to know with certainty what was engraved between the flailing limbs – the degree of explicitness. Instead there is just a set of pen and ink drawings, made much later by Count de Waldeck, that appear to be copies from the original set of Raimondi prints. It is from these copies that we can see a more complete picture of the original engravings.

Looking at the prints, it is not hard to see why the engravings caused such a furore in the first place. The level of explicitness was without parallel, and was reinforced by the degree of detail made possible by the development of copperplate engraving. More than that, this was sex in its own right. It was as remarkable for what it didn't show as for what it did. At a time when the theme 'Loves of the Gods' was popular with Renaissance painters, there was little if any overt classical allusion here. Any moral and religious framework once glued in place by the Middle Ages had come unstuck; any classical allusion was so flimsy as to be useless. It is hard to see in these designs anything other than vigorous and athletic sex. This was a complete reversal of the value system that had been in operation since the beginnings of the Church. This was no longer God at the centre and man at the edges bearing the shame of sexual desire as a result of the Fall. God had left the frame, leaving man at the centre, vigorously asserting his right to engage in sex for sex's sake. It is this that has led several commentators to see in the *Postures* the first example of pornography that would be recognized as such today. As Clifford Scheiner, who is a dealer in erotic books, says, 'What I find most interesting about the illustrations is that the images are extremely modern. People today somehow think that they discovered sex, or that sex in the twentieth century is different from sex previously. They're very, very mistaken. When you have two naked people engaged in intercourse or sexual activity, what was documented as happening in the 1520s is exactly what goes on in the bedrooms of the 1990s.'[19]

Worse than the content of the engravings, however, was the audience. Raimondi's chief transgression was not so much what he engraved as to whom he made it available. While Giulio Romano, the original artist, was commended at the time because 'he did not expose it in the public squares or in the churches', Raimondi by contrast was rebuked for being he 'who for his own profit engraved them'.[20] Romano got away with it and Raimondi didn't. Romano retained the confidence of the Pope and flourished at the court of Duke Federico di Gonzaga in Mantua and Raimondi was thrown into jail. Why? Again we see the social disquiet raised by the possibilities of print. There was no act of private patronage to redeem the engravings. There was no closed circle around which they could circulate. This was a production blindly offered as a commercial proposition. As Paula Findlen, professor of history at Stanford University, says, 'The problem for Raimondi was exactly the problem of print; the problem of circulating images to anyone who could buy them, circulating them in the marketplace is one of the fundamental reasons why Raimondi is in trouble and Romano is not.'[21]

But that was not the end of the story. One of the most infamous and scurrilous of

◁ Count de Waldeck's drawings (*c.*1858) of the original Raimondi engravings. The de Waldeck copies are our only source for knowing what the original engravings might have looked like.

writers, Pietro Aretino (1492–1557), known variously as the 'Teller of Truth', the 'Divine Aretino', the 'Scourge of Princes', the 'Scourge of Pricks' and the 'Pimp to Popes', saw the engravings, 'was touched by the same inspiration which moved Giulio Romano to draw them', and so penned a sonnet to go with each sexual position. Subsequently the sonnets were published with woodcut prints of the engravings in book form in 1527. Once more, there was a huge scandal. As Vasari says, 'I know not which is the greater, the offence to the eye from the drawings of Giulio, or the outrage to the ear from the words of Aretino.'[22]

The reason for all the fuss? The most obvious explanation is in the verses themselves, which are written in alternate male and female voices. Take this example from Sonnet 5:

> Put your leg on my shoulder,
> And stick my cock in your cunt,
> And while I gently move in and out,
> Draw me tightly to your breast.
>
> And if I slip from cunt to arse,
> Call me whatever vile names you wish,
> Since I know that difference as well
> As a stallion knows what to do with a mare in heat.
>
> My hand will keep your cock in place,
> Lest it slip, but you'd know that
> By the dirty look on my face.
>
> They say only one enjoys a bum-fuck,
> While it's shared enjoyment the other way,
> So let's do it that way, and quickly.
>
> Like Hell, my dear, I'm in no rush,
> I wouldn't leave this screwing
> Even to save the King of France.[23]

△ Aretino's Sonnet 4 to accompany a woodcut of Posture 4, printed in 1527.

To Raimondi's outrageous act, Aretino had added his own act of transgression, putting man, putting sex at the centre. It is not God who gives life meaning but fucking. As Aretino says in Sonnet 1:

> Fuck me, dearest, one quick fuck,
> Since we were born to fuck,
> And you adore cock, like I love cunt,
> And a world without cock play is a meaningless nothing.

◁▽ Heliogravures from 1892 of the *Postures*. The *Postures* were to exercise a strong influence, and variations on Raimondi's original engravings were to be reproduced and copied down through the ages.

And again, in Sonnet 2:

> It is a foolish dim wit
> Who doesn't realize it a waste of time
> Unless a thing concerns fucking.[24]

Aretino outlined his reasons for penning the sonnets: 'I reject the furtive attitude and filthy custom which forbids the eyes what delights them most. What harm is there in seeing a man mount a woman? Should the beasts be more free than us?'[25] And, 'We should wear that thing nature gave us for the preservation of the species on a chain around our necks or as a medal on our hats . . .'[26] This was a conscious rejection of the false modesty and artificial airs and hypocritical conventions. As Aretino was to put it, in the words of a prostitute in one of his other works, discussing how to be a successful whore, 'Speak plainly and say "fuck", "prick", "cunt" and "arse" . . . Why don't you say it straight out and stop going about on tiptoes?'[27]

For Clifford Scheiner, the book containing Aretino's sonnets marked 'a turning point in Western civilization, because this is the earliest example we have where people printed erotic text and married it

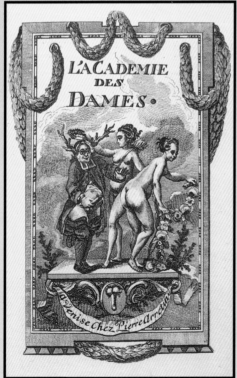

with erotic illustration and did it in such a way that it was widely available'.[28] The only known edition of the book disappeared altogether after 1800, but then re-emerged in 1927. When Scheiner was later given the chance to purchase it he was thrilled: 'When you find something that's lost, it's a huge excitement. It's like a hundred birthdays rolled into one. You can look at it, you can hold it, you can see how the sewing is done. You had all the years of excitement, the expectation, and here it's come to fruition.'

So, the notoriety and attempted suppression of Aretino's *Postures* secured their place in history. It is the familiar dynamic. As Walter Kendrick says, 'The establishment of a restricted area is itself the boldest invitation to trespass.'[29] In other words, censorship itself goes some way to creating what it seeks to control: the transgressive and the repressive are but two sides of the same coin. We have come across this before. The more successful the repression, the rarer the object and the more desired and precious it becomes. The immediate attempt at repressing the *Postures* was as successful as an act of censorship could hope to be: the original plates were destroyed and there is only one (incomplete) version of the 1527 book still in existence. And yet this very success, the very rarity, spawned a fetishization of the book among collectors, and much of the erotic imagery produced in Western Europe was an imitation of the sixteen postures and sonnets. There were new editions, new translations, new inauthentic verses and inauthentic illustrations: new editions appeared in Venice in 1556 and 1779, Paris in 1757 and 1882, Rome in 1792, Lieden in 1864, Brussels in 1865, and Berlin in 1904.[30] In the nineteenth century at least one brothel boasted paintings of Aretino's *Postures* on its walls;[31] and the Earl of Rochester's *Farce of Sodom* (c.1680) is set in an 'Antechamber hung round with Aretino's *Postures*'. In 1674 students at All Souls College, Oxford, attempted to print their own secret edition of Aretino's *Postures*, using the University press at night, and Ben Jonson mentions the *Postures* in his play *The Alchemist*.[32] Even brothels would be advertised with the Aretine name.

By creating rules as to what could and could not be shown in terms of sex, the sexual image had been invested with political power. A process that had started with the problematization of sex in early Christianity and continued with the marginalization of sex throughout the Middle Ages was consolidated in the strictures of the Counter-Reformation. Obscenity was subversive; flouting the rules became a political act.

From the sixteenth century there was a series of books detailing sexual exploits that, in the Aretine tradition, seemed to share the philosophy (albeit sometimes with a veneer of moralizing) that sexual desire and pleasure were desirable ends in themselves: books like *La Puttana errante* (1531), *L'Ecole des Filles* (*ou La Philosophie des Dames*) (1655), *L'Académie des Dames* (1660), *Histoire de Dom Bougre* (*ou Le Portier des Chartreux*) (1741), *Thérèse Philosophe* (1748), *Memoirs of a Woman of Pleasure* (also known as *Fanny Hill*) by John Cleland (1748–9). They were often bought by gentlemen and confined to relatively small educated circles. In 1668 Samuel Pepys recorded in his diary that he bought a copy of *L'Ecole des Filles*:

> Thence away to the Strand to my bookseller's, and there stayed an hour and bought that idle, roguish book, L'escholle des Fille; which I have bought in plain binding (avoiding the buying of it better bound) because I resolve, as soon as I

◁ (Top left) *Histoire de Dom Bougre (ou Le Portier des Chartreux)*, 1741. (Top right) *Thérèse Philosophe*, 1783 (Vol II). (Bottom, left and right) *L'Académie des Dames*, 1680.

▽▷ (Top) *Le Religeux*, 1740. (Bottom) *'J'arrive . . . Je Suis la Bonne Constitution'*. From the seventeenth century, sexual satire was used as a weapon against both religious and secular authorities.

have read it, to burn it, that it may not stand in the list of books, nor among them, to disgrace them if it should be found.[33]

He then recorded – albeit in code and in a passage that has frequently been left out of the published editions of his diaries – that he masturbated: 'It was a mighty lewd book … but it did hazer my prick para stand all the while, and una vez to decharger.' After which, he threw the book on the fire.

Much as the implicit libertine philosophy in these books was at odds with conventional Christian morality, their subversiveness was muted and their readership harmless. But this was not always the case, as history soon demonstrated.

From the seventeenth century sexual satire was used as a weapon against both religious and secular authorities. The period coincided with a huge rise in printing houses and in commercial opportunities for selling printed material in the marketplace. Much of this literature was ephemeral and has not been handed down, but its prevalence is indicated by news reports like that of 13 October 1696 which referred to the burning of a 'cart load' of obscene publications and cards 'tending to promote debauchery'. The Catholic Church and the Pope were the frequent butt of obscene polemical literature, but the genre was also used against other religious groups, from the Puritans to the Quakers and Methodists. The use of obscene literature was particularly

evident at times of political stress, and the Restoration period (1660–85) saw a flurry of attacks against the perceived absolutist ambitions of the monarch. The threat of tyranny was frequently seen in sexual terms, with Charles II's sceptre portrayed as a rampaging penis.

But nowhere was political pornography more on view and with more dramatic effect than in the French Revolution. As Lynn Hunt, professor of history at the University of Pennsylvania, says, 'Politically motivated pornography helped to bring about the Revolution by undermining the legitimacy of the ancien régime as a social and political system.'[34] In one tract entitled 'L'Autrichienne en gouguettes' as soon as the King passes out drunk, he is cuckolded by his brother the Conte d'Artois and then by the Duchesse de Polignac. Another variation on the same theme was the sexual exploits of the Queen with her valet, the King's brother and deputy Le Chapelier together.[35]

By portraying Marie Antoinette as a whore, a lesbian, an adulteress, a pervert and

△ *'Suite de portrait de la reine.'* These 'composite heads' were popular in attacking not only the monarchy, as shown here, but also the aristocracy.

an incestuous debauchee, this literature was challenging the legitimacy of her rule. In fact, as Lynn Hunt has suggested, there is an implicit revolutionary logic here that strikes at the heart of the monarchy[36]: if she was a tart who would spread her legs for all and sundry – including her valet – then who could guarantee that the King was the father of her children? And if paternity could not be guaranteed, what of the claims for the royal lineage? And if the lineage was in doubt, what of the legitimacy of the monarchy? The message was clear: if any man could be her lover, any man could be king.

It was not just the Queen who was being attacked. For instance, the 'composite heads' of aristocrats and clerics showed their heads made up of copulating couples and genitals. Their lofty pretensions were being punctured; whatever authority they might have assumed for themselves was being demystified. The reductionism is an invitation to see the 'high' in terms of the 'low'. And once this happens, authority evaporates. The treatment was also extended to other political figures, as in *Les Enfans de Sodomie à l'Assemblée Nationale* (1790). It was a process that degraded the exalted, as it elevated the common man.

To add insult to injury, the aristocracy and royalty were not just attacked as licentious debauchees, but were simultaneously portrayed as impotent, frail and ravaged by venereal diseases. This was double jeopardy: they suffered not only the ignominy of being cast in degrading pornographic roles but also the additional humiliation of being considered unequal to them.

What had started out as a scurrilous and often vicious sexual satire passed around by libertine upper classes among themselves developed into something altogether more worrying. Ribald attacks – even the most unpleasant – confined to a small circle was one

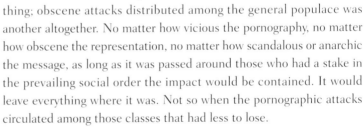

thing; obscene attacks distributed among the general populace was another altogether. No matter how vicious the pornography, no matter how obscene the representation, no matter how scandalous or anarchic the message, as long as it was passed around those who had a stake in the prevailing social order the impact would be contained. It would leave everything where it was. Not so when the pornographic attacks circulated among those classes that had less to lose.

Pornography was a runaway success. It has been estimated that by the end of the ancien régime two-thirds of all printed literature being read in France was forbidden, and a large amount of this was pornographic. The bustling trade in pornographic tracts was centred at the Palais Royal. One royalist commentator even complained that the outrageous pamphlets against the Queen were sold under the King's window. The tracts and pamphlets were written by *'des rousseaux des ruisseaux'* or 'gutter philosophers', produced by printers on the Left Bank and smuggled over the river by street hawkers. These hawkers would lurk in arcades and passageways, spreading out their wares –

tiny books and tracts – when they could and then bundling them away immediately the police appeared. It was a huge trade, with something like 300 street hawkers operating in and around the Palais Royal. And unlike the pornography of the ancien régime, which was often expensively bound and was circulated among the well-to-do, these tracts were affordable to a significant proportion of the population. Publications became shorter and more accessible. This was not pornography to be enjoyed by the privileged in private but brash texts designed to be shared aloud in public.

The early days of the French Revolution were perhaps the last time pornography was used as a principal vehicle of political expression. The nature of pornography seemed to change between the very end of the eighteenth and the beginning of the nineteenth centuries. From that time pornography took on less overtly political forms, although its ability to turn things upside down was not forgotten, and it would be shadowed by a sense of danger and subversion.

From the start of the nineteenth century the State took an increasing interest in the publication of pornography, culminating in England in the passing of the Obscene Publications Act in 1857. For instance, the publication of that widely read pornographic novel, *Fanny Hill*, in 1748–49 prompted no interest on the part of the British government; a century later the book was banned.

That pornographic literature was seen as dangerous – something that needed to be controlled and monitored – is further indicated by the establishment of the secret museums of the print world in the nineteenth century: for example, the Enfer at the Bibliothèque Nationale in Paris and the Private Case at the British Library in London. At the British Library, this contained books that were not listed as part of the general catalogue (and would not be until the 1960s); nor indeed was there any printed list to tell readers of its existence. As one article published in December 1913 in the *English Review*, under the title 'Taboos of the British Museum Library', noted, there were three categories of book liable to be excluded from the general catalogue: books subversive to the throne, books subversive to religion and books of an improper or obscene character.

But while the nineteenth century preoccupied itself with the lessons of the past, the future of pornography lay elsewhere. Print would continue to occupy centre stage for those increasingly concerned with the problem of obscenity well into the twentieth century, but a brand-new pornographic medium was already waiting in the wings and it would ultimately have the greater impact: it was photography.

△ *Fanny Hill* (*c*.1923). The original caption reads: 'Fanny's beauties displayed'.

◁ Scene of sodomy between deputies to the National Assembly. From *Les Enfans de Sodome – l'Assemblée Nationale* (Paris, 1790). The text reads: 'This masculine trio, with its ingenious tastes, recalls for you the readers the games of true buggers.'

The Mechanical Eye

[Chapter Four: Photography]

A rather remarkable thing happened in the nineteenth century: pictures of naked women became scandalous. Ever since the Renaissance, the nude had been not only accepted but venerated. Not merely one of several subjects available to the artist, she was increasingly *the* subject, the testing ground for an aspiring painter, the mark of a great artist. Nudes were synonymous with fine art and high culture, masterpieces of the Western tradition: Botticelli's *The Birth of Venus* (c.1478), Correggio's *Danaë* (c.1531), Tintoretto's *Susannah and the Elders* (c.1555), Rubens' *Three Graces* (c.1640), Titian's *Venus and the Organ Player* (c.1548) – all of them nudes.

In his influential work *The Nude*, the eminent twentieth-century art historian Kenneth Clark makes an important distinction between 'naked' and 'the nude', putting it like this:

> It is widely supposed that the naked human body is in itself an object upon which the eye dwells with pleasure and which we are glad to see depicted. But anyone who has frequented art schools and seen the shapeless, pitiful model which the students are industriously drawing will know that this is an illusion . . . We do not wish to imitate; we wish to perfect.[1]

Naked was the body deprived of clothes; the nude was the body clothed by art.[2] Naked was a 'huddled, defenceless body' and the nude 'the body re-formed'. The nude was the transformation of a naked woman into art.

◁ Anonymous, c.1885.

△ *The Birth of Venus*
(1863) by Alexandre
Cabanal (1823–89). This
was shown at the Paris
Salon of 1863; a
confection whose
popularity at the time
revealed an idealized taste
in art that often found
nude photography
unpalatable.

And yet in the middle of the nineteenth century, pictures of naked females were provoking not admiration but anguish. 'This is one thing we cannot look upon without disgust,' commented one writer, while others complained of pictures 'boldly showing insolent details', of 'poses that attracted looks and excited the senses', of 'the simple offence to the eye' and of 'sad nudities'.

When was a nude not a nude? When she was a photograph. The pictures that were causing such wringing of hands, such gnashing of teeth were *photographs*. What was a nude in the hands of an artist became naked in the hands of a photographer. Clark's nude was transformed back to the shapeless, pitiful model she had always been and, newly naked, she became indecent. The photographic nude, it seems, was an impossibility, a contradiction in terms.

Outrage alone, no matter how forcibly expressed, tells us little about the images themselves, but even if we allow for the possibility that the photographic images were more explicit than their painted sisters, we still do not have the whole story. There was something troubling about the very category 'photographic nude'. When the new Société française de Photographie organized its first major exhibition in the summer of 1855, it was made clear that 'nudes in general, and without exception, will be refused'.[3] *Any* photographic nude was problematic.

If we compare Titian's painting of *Venus Anadyomene* (c.1522) with Darnay's photograph of Augustine Guy (1858), on page 97, we may well wonder what was so

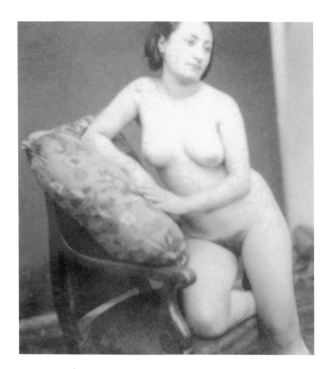

troubling. The positions of the bodies are similar enough, the amounts of flesh on view are the same, the looks indistinguishable, the backgrounds unremarkable. And yet the Titian was a revered masterpiece while Darnay's photograph was seized by the Paris police in a raid that landed Darnay in prison.[4] The distinction between the painted and the photographic nude was a puzzling one and sixty years later the authorities were still wrestling with it. On 13 February 1914 *The Times* reported:

> Recently in Berlin a large number of [photographic] picture post-cards, representing classical pictures, were seized by the police on the ground that they were indecent, and their action was upheld by the Provisional Court of Berlin. This decision, however, was quashed by the Supreme Court of Justice at Leipzig, the President of which ordered, 'That it was inadmissible to declare a picture indecent because it represented a naked body.'

△ (Left) *Augustine Guy,* 1858, attributed to M. Darnay. This photograph was seized and confiscated by the French police. (Right) *Venus Anadyomene* (*c.*1522) by Titian. This painting was revered as a masterpiece.

And, even more puzzling, in 1881 in Hamburg, photographic reproductions of Titian's Venuses and other paintings were confiscated as obscene.[5] What was art in the gallery was not art in the streets. The difference, it seemed, was not the content but the medium itself. The question is this: what was it about the new technology of photography that threatened to topple art into obscenity?

Photography had not always provoked such hostility. When Louis Daguerre first unveiled his invention, which he called a daguerreotype, it was hailed as a triumph. In an enthusiastic presentation by Dominique Arago to the French Chamber of Deputies on 3 July 1839, the full advantages of the wondrous new process were spelled out. First, it

△ *Académie* figure, c.1870. Photographer: Guglielmo Marconi.

could be used by anyone: 'When, step by step, a few simple prescribed rules are followed, there is no one who cannot succeed as certainly and as well as can M. Daguerre himself.' It could achieve 'unimaginable precision' of detail. And, what 'probably astonished the public more than anything else', there was its sheer speed: 'In fact, scarcely ten or twelve minutes are required for photographing a monument, a section of a town, or a scene, even in dull, winter weather.'⁶ Daguerre's invention was bought by the French state and Daguerre was awarded a pension for life.

The daguerreotype was based on the old idea of the camera obscura, a darkened chamber or small building in which images of outside objects are projected on to a flat surface by a convex lens in an aperture. It had been known since the sixteenth century that by pointing a box with a small pinhole at an object, the light rays would travel through the hole and form an inverted image at the back of the box, but it was not clear how to fix that image. When it was realized that certain chemical elements responded to light in different ways, the challenge – which Daguerre was to meet – was to find the right chemical medium to record in a convincing and accurate way the variations of light.

Daguerre's achievement caused a sensation, but the secret process was kept under wraps until it was revealed for the first time at a special meeting of l'Académie des Sciences in August 1839. Eyewitness accounts convey something of the fevered atmosphere at the event:

> Gradually I managed to push through the crowd … after a long wait a door opens in the background, and the first of the audience to come out rush into the vestibule. 'Silver iodide,' cries one, 'Quicksilver,' shouts another, while a third maintains that hyposulphite of soda is the name of the secret substance … An hour later, all the opticians' shops were besieged, but could not rake together enough instruments to satisfy the on-rushing army of would-be daguerreotypists;

a few days later you could see in all the squares of Paris three-legged dark-boxes planted in front of churches and palaces …[7]

Then came Daguerre's first public demonstration of his new process. A camera obscura was lined up in front of a window in view of the Tuileries; the silver-coated side of a copper plate was polished, painted with iodine and placed at the back of the camera obscura. After a wait of fifteen minutes, the plate was removed and coated with globules of hot mercury and then washed with solution. And there, sure enough, and to general acclaim, was a small and perfectly detailed picture of the Tuileries and the Seine.[8]

The camera was a machine for the nineteenth century. Along with railroads, the telegraph and mass production, it spelled progress, the harnessing of nature for the improvement of man's condition. It was the symbol of the modern age – a technical triumph for a new industrial world. Edgar Allan Poe wrote breathlessly, 'The instrument itself must undoubtedly be regarded as the most important, and perhaps most extraordinary, triumph of modern science.'[9]

And it was not just a victory for science. What Daguerre succeeded in doing was what many took to be the dream of art: to produce pictures so exact that they looked real. This had been the conventional goal of Western art down the centuries and is vividly revealed in Pliny's story of the ancient Greeks, Parrhasius and Zeuxis, who entered into a competition to see which of them was the finer artist. Zeuxis painted grapes so realistically that the birds flew down to eat from the painted vine. Proud of such an artistic coup, he invited Parrhasius to draw back the curtain on his picture to see if it could match such an achievement. When Zeuxis realized that the curtain *was* the picture, he conceded defeat, saying that whereas he had succeeded only in fooling the birds, Parrhasius had fooled an artist.[10]

With such illusionism as an ideal, surely art was doomed, for how could the artist compete with this new technology? Speaking about photography, the American Samuel Morse declared, 'The exquisite minuteness of the delineation cannot be conceived. No painting or engraving ever approached it.' The invention caused despair among some artists, the French painter Paul Delaroche (1797–1856) announcing, 'From today painting is dead.' Not everyone was so beguiled, though, and the blind, mechanical processes of photography struck many as the very antithesis of art. The influential artists turned novelists Edmond and Jules de Goncourt, for example, described the photographer as a blind man with a camera 'who stops to sit down [and take a picture] wherever there is a dunghill'.[11]

For a medium that was quick to attempt to reproduce the classic images of art, it was inevitable that the nude – the naked woman – would also be a subject. However, the immediate problem with any kind of portraiture was exposure time. Despite Daguerre's proud boast that an

▽ Distributed as a photographic *académie*, 1854, Jacques Antoine Moulin, *Photographic Studies*. As Anne McCauley points out, from the beginning the female body was erotically encoded in photography.

△ Nude, 1849, Gustave Le Gray, from the *Album Regnault*. A genuine use of the photographic image as an artist's *aide-mémoire*.

image could be produced in 'three to thirty minutes at the most', attempting to sit for twenty-minute sessions in a studio in blasting sunshine under glass with ingenious paraphernalia to keep the head and body still tested both the sitters and the technology to the limit. It was not until 'accelerators' allowed the whole process to speed up that portraiture became possible.

And sure enough, soon after the first portraits came the first daguerreotypes of naked women. In Paris, the earliest legal nude images were the so-called '*académies*'. These were supposedly academic studies, similar to the drawings an artist would be expected to make from live models as part of his training; they were something that was allowed as an *aide-mémoire* to save the expense of hiring the models. With such a front of respectability, they could be legitimately sold. In practice, however, these '*académies*' did not always look very 'academic' and, often cropped mid-thigh or mid-shoulder, with bits of clothing and elaborate props, their usefulness as an artistic tool was doubtless limited. The props give it away, as Abigail Solomon-Godeau says, 'Once you start seeing all these props, the stockings, the garters, the shoes, the jewellery, it's perfectly evident that the body is being coded for its erotic appeal. These are codes that make the viewer aware that this is a body that is intended for erotic consumption.'[12]

In one of the early issues of the first photographic journal, *La Lumière*, the following ad appeared:

DAGUERREOTYPE – Portraits de jolies femmes, et sujets de fantasie pour montres – Etudes d'après nature pour artistes – MOULIN, 31 bis, Rue de Faubourg-Montmartre – Expédie en province et à l'étranger.[13]

◁ *Academic Study – No. 6,*
1854, Bruno Braquehais.

It is common among today's enthusiasts and collectors of these rare and valuable daguerreotypes to see something sensual about the very medium itself. A velvety radiance is created by the precious metals contained in it and the mirror-like qualities require that it be seen at the right distance and in the right light, and demand attention and careful handling that make it all the more precious. Uwe Scheid has the largest single collection of erotic daguerreotypes in the world. As a collector of 'pornography', he occupies unstable ground, being part expert, part voyeur and part consumer. Pornography is not neutral territory. To study it, to collect it, to write about it, even to condemn it, all involve an act of looking that implicates the student, collector, writer or critic. Scheid, however, is happy to accept that the principal motive for his collection is pleasure – pleasure, he readily admits, that involves sensual pleasure: 'Daguerreotypes have an altogether special aura – they have a richness and range of tonal values that fascinate me. They emanate a quite particular glow that is hard to describe, but if you hold a daguerreotype up you are really aware of it.'[14]

△ Daguerreotype,
anonymous, *c.*1855.

▷ (Top left)
Anonymous, *c.*1865.
(Top right)
Anonymous, *c.*1860.
(Bottom left)
Anonymous, *c.*1885.
(Bottom right)
Anonymous, *c.*1890.
All from the Uwe Scheid
Collection.

Most of the Scheid collection comprises stereo daguerreotypes. By the time the accelerators were sufficiently developed to cope with the nude, there was a new craze: the stereoscope. By using a camera with two lenses, two pictures could be taken simultaneously, side by side, reproducing the views of the left and the right eyes. When the pictures were placed in a special viewer, the left eye would focus on the image on the left and the right eye would focus on the image on the right, and together they created a startling three-dimensional effect. Many of the first nude daguerreotypes were made for the stereoscope. These were 'virtual reality' images before their time, and the erotic or pornographic image in a stereoscope gave a viewing experience that had been quite unavailable before. Enthusiasts today often describe their first experience as a Road to Damascus. Uwe Scheid, for example, was a camera collector when he stumbled on his first erotic daguerreotype: 'I must say, it was such a fascinating experience. I was so terribly excited when I first held stereo nude daguerreotypes and experienced the whole thing in three dimensions. People look like they are standing alive in front of you: they are so close you feel you could touch them. It was sensational for me. The whole night afterwards, I couldn't sleep. It was incredible.'

Not everyone approved. As Baudelaire observed in 1862:

It was not long before thousands of pairs of greedy eyes were glued to the peepholes of the stereoscope, as though they were the skylights of the infinite. The love of obscenity, which is as vigorous a growth in the heart of natural man as self-love, could not let slip such a glorious opportunity for its own satisfaction ... I once heard a smart woman, not of my society, say to her friends, who were discreetly trying to hide such pictures from her, thus taking it upon themselves to have some modesty on her behalf, 'Let me see; nothing shocks me.' That is what she said, I swear it, I heard it with my own ears; but who will believe me?[15]

At first, the daguerreotypes reached a restricted public, and the erotic images were really an illicit luxury for the wealthy gentleman, the secret erotic toy of nineteenth-century male élites. The daguerreotype is a one-off; the plate that is developed is unique, an original 'positive' image. With the laborious preparation and materials necessary to produce a single picture, it was not cheap. In 1845, prices for daguerreotype portraits ranged from one to two guineas. For most ordinary working people, this would be a month's pay.

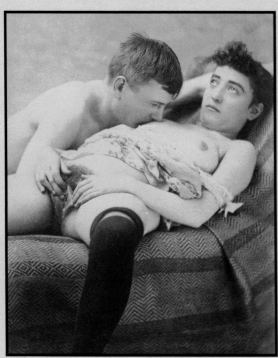

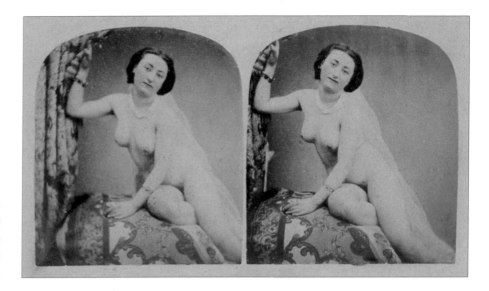

▷ Anonymous, *c.*1858.
The stereoscope was able
to produce remarkable
three-dimensional
images.

▽ Daguerreotype.
Anonymous, *c.*1855. A
number of the early
daguerreotypes
reproduced classical
poses, like the 'Three
Graces'.

A great democratizing blow for photography came with the development of the wet-plate process, which allowed an efficient system of developing 'negatives' that could be turned into 'positives' by printing them on albumen-coated paper. Unlimited numbers of prints could be run off relatively cheaply. As the prices of the photographic image plummeted, it was possible to buy a portrait for a tenth of the cost of an old daguerreotype.

Suddenly cheap prints were available everywhere, as indeed were cheap stereo pictures: 'No home is complete without a stereoscope,' announced one advertisement for the London Stereoscope Co. Equally, in France, the production of *académies* soared. Photographic prints were required to be registered at the Ministry of the Interior of the Préfecture of Police in 1852 and virtually immediately the *académies* accounted for nearly half of the images registered for public sale in the 1850s. Such popularity suggests that it was not just art students who were buying them. As with the magazines for 'art photographers' that were produced in the early twentieth century, many supposed *académies* were just soft-core by another name.

Whether because of conventional expectations, artistic ambition or as a cover for more cynical motives, many of these early images of naked women employed the full and familiar range of symbols of high art. Visual classical references: the column, the pose, the curtain. These were the codes that Western art had so carefully evolved in performing its delicate balancing act of making sex acceptable within art – to contain the erotic within accepted and recognized boundaries. The sex in these paintings was kept at arm's length by idealizing the nude, often by putting the model in a mythical setting.

◁ Académie, *c.*1858,
Braquehais.

But photographers were to discover that the same techniques did not automatically transform their images into art or confer respectability. Indeed, sometimes they merely succeeded in inviting ridicule.

As one professional journal in England said at the time, 'In painted pictures the columns appear plausible, but the manner in which they are applied to photography is absurd, for they usually stand on a rug. But as everyone knows, marble or stone columns are not commonly built with carpet as their base.'

The problem with photography was that it was too candid; it showed too much. And a surfeit of the real made it impossible to sustain the ideal. Instead of the painter's ability to idealize the human form, in a photograph the blemishes and the imperfections of the actual woman were on full view. Instead of the alabaster skins, there were blemished ones; instead of idealized limbs, there were awkward, foreshortened ones; nymph's

▷ Anonymous *c.*1875.

breasts would be replaced by disappointing real ones. 'As ugly as a daguerreotype,' became a standard quip, and, as one writer put it, 'They [stereograms] seldom or ever include any female who approaches in the remotest degree to a Venus ...' According to Catholic commentator Louis Veuillot:

> I am talking about the simple offence to the eye. The assemblages that are produced aren't content to have ugly faces, most to the point of abjection; they are at the same time generally and in diverse ways extremely badly built; knock-kneed, heavy jowled, potbellied, bent over, bony, impudent and gauche, knowing neither how to walk nor stand up.[16]

More disturbing than this, however, was that the viewer was directly confronted by the reality of the women who were being photographed – not some imagined Venus, but, no doubt, a washerwoman or, worse, a prostitute. In French police files, the occupations of those models who were arrested in connection with the sale of 'obscene subjects' were '*fleuriste*' and '*lingère*'.[17] From police records we also know that many of these photographs were produced in the working-class district of Belleville. Not a goddess, then, but ... a *working-class* woman.

As one writer in an edition of *Photographic News* (1858) wrote:

> We are not shocked at the sight of a Cupid without pantaloons – not hypercritically fastidious about the pose of a Venus or a Hercules; but to see a too life-like representation of courtezanship transferred in all its faithful hideousness

to picture tablets by photo-actinism – a very microcosm of impurity – this is one thing we cannot look upon without disgust … to our mind there is something positively sacrilegious in the idea of prostituting the light of heaven to such debasing purposes.

For another:

> In the case of those lithographs which were a disgrace to human nature, there was at least the consolation of knowing that they had no existence except in the salacious imagination of some immoral draughtsman, who prostitutes his talents to so vile and degrading a purpose; while in the slides we are alluding to we have full assurance that a woman has been the model.[18]

This was the shock of the real. Beyond the disdain expressed for the imperfections, beyond the derision prompted by the clumsy props and beyond the ridicule reserved for the forced mannerisms and grimaces lay the basic human reaction to the recognition that this was a real naked woman (and it was almost exclusively a woman rather than a man in the early days), someone who could be walking down the street right now or someone you could visit in a brothel round the corner. Unlike in a painting, where the viewer's relationship with the artist's model was mediated and distanced by the artist's vision to such an extent that the real person – if indeed there ever was one – dropped out of view, in a photograph the viewer was afforded no such distance. And the recognition of this new dynamic prompted a different kind of reaction: one of revulsion, or complicity, or pleasure, or arousal – or a mixture of all four.

▽ Daguerreotype, anonymous, *c.*1855. Images of naked women were made as soon as it was possible to capture portraits with the new daguerreotype process. There was deep ambivalence about these new nudes which brought with them the shock of the real.

This is the uniqueness of the photograph. When Roland Barthes was trying to search for the essence of photography, he found it here: 'One day, quite some time ago, I happened on a photograph of Napoleon's youngest brother, Jérome, taken in 1852. And I realized then, with an amazement I have not been able to lessen since: "I am looking at eyes that looked at the Emperor."'[19] And, 'Here are some Polish soldiers resting in a field [André Kertész, 1915]; nothing extraordinary, except this, which no realist painting would give me, that *they were there*.'[20] Less accessibly, if more precisely, Abigail Solomon-Godeau says, 'The photograph's direct and causal linkage to its referent determines its ontological difference from other iconic systems.'[21] And in his *A Short History of Photography*, Walter Benjamin says, 'In photography … one encounters something strange and new … something that is not to be silenced, something demanding the name of the person who had lived then, who even now is still real and will never entirely perish into *art*.'[22]

▷ Anonymous, *c.*1885.

The photograph suggests a connection between the viewer and the person viewed that does not exist in art. *I* am looking at *this* person. The realm of painting allows an indeterminacy between the viewer and the person viewed that the photograph does not. This is new and distinct. Photography is a medium that creates a different set of connections between the person who produces the work, the person who is present in the work and the person who sees the work.

Photography, then, was not simply a new means of representing the human body; it in fact represented a shift in social connections. What was often so shocking to nineteenth-century viewers was that these connections were *vulgar*: they had a whiff of the common. The class disdain in discussions of photography is particularly apparent in the distaste for photographic nudes: in France in 1862, one contemporary bemoaned 'those sad nudities which display with a desperate truth all the physical and moral ugliness of the models paid by the session'.[23] In 1857 the comic magazine *Le Triboulet* commented on these 'hideous' and 'stupid' nudes, 'the models for which seem to be selected in the most heavily trafficked establishments in Paris'.[24] Gabriel Pelin, complaining of the open display of these images in showcases, says, 'Who had not seen the noble faces of virgins and empresses exposed pell-mell beside nude courtesans? ... People not only sell obscene photographs ... Certain merchants even give the address of the model!'[25] It is almost as if the very act of looking implicated and debased the spectator, threatening, as it did, to connect them with the wrong kind – the lower kind, the dirty kind – of person.

Real women. Real bodies. Real sex. The association of vulgarity could extend to those who were buying the photographs and those who were distributing them. As Lady Elizabeth Eastlake noted in the *London Quarterly Review*:

> Who can number the legion of petty dabblers, who display their trays of specimens along every great thoroughfare in London, executing for our lowest servants, for one shilling, that which no money could have commanded for the Rothschild bride of twenty years ago?[26]

Photography was something of a social upstart, attempting to appropriate the codes of 'high culture' for those who had no rightful or natural inheritance. Art had been that definitive area of taste and judgement that allowed the privileged classes to distinguish themselves from the commoner classes. How could art perform such a function of social distinction if it was subsumed by photography, something that, in Daguerre's words, 'anyone can do'? It was this that lay behind the persistence and hysteria of the endless debates about the relative merits of photography and art. The portrait, for instance, had always been the preserve of the well-to-do: to commission a painted portrait required money; it was one of the badges of social standing. As the development of print had been before it, these new photographic portraits – which all echelons of society desired to own – were a levelling force; as the common man or woman was elevated, so the upper classes were diminished by the democratizing tendency of the camera lens, which could not be relied upon to distinguish the noble from the ignoble.

Photography's relative cheapness after the development of the wet-plate process fuelled the industry in pornographic photographs. Elizabeth Anne McCauley has pieced together a picture that tells of the sheer scale of the industry by going through the archives of the Paris Préfecture, established in 1855 to record the arrests, booty and details of the suspects. In 1858 M. Darnay, twenty-seven years old, was arrested with his accomplices, a travelling salesman, a hand-tinter and five girls, the oldest of whom was eighteen. Darnay had been under surveillance for some time when a police officer

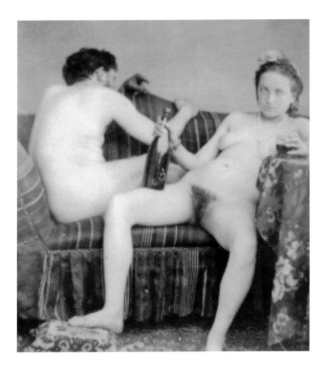

△ One of the confiscated images (1862) in the files of the Paris police; the file states that the girl in the photograph, 'Sophie', was a twenty-year-old machinist. The archives were established in 1855.

bought sixty francs' worth of goods. He got fifteen months, his male accomplices six months and the girls one month in prison. Philip Dubourjal, a thirty-year-old wine merchant and photographer, was arrested first in 1859. He had 1,748 obscene prints in his possession when he was arrested for a second time in 1860. When Joseph Auguste Belloc's hand-colourist's was raided in October 1861, police found 1,200 obscene photographs in the darkroom, some 3,000 prints on paper, 307 negatives, four albums of photographs of nude women and 102 large-format prints of women in 'licentious positions'. Alexandre Bertrand had two dozen daguerreotypes, thirty-two negatives and 206 prints seized and labelled 'licentious' when the police raided his studio on the rue Dauphine in 1860. In 1864, M. and Mme Lamarre, who ran a shop selling toys, crystals and photographs, were arrested in Nantes for dealing in obscene images. They had hidden fourteen photographs in a locked wardrobe and in addition police seized forty-three photographs in the shop window. They were sentenced to prison for forty days, with a fine of 100 francs.[27]

No case in McCauley's researches quite matched that of pornographer Henry Hayler of Pimlico Road, London. In 1874 the Society for the Prevention of Vice brought a prosecution for the destruction of a haul totalling 130,248 photographs and 5,000 slides which had been seized. Hayler escaped his summons by disappearing. He and his wife and family feature in the photographs themselves, and he was said to have been involved in this kind of trade for years. The solicitor for the Society for the Prevention of Vice, a Mr Collette, declared it 'the grossest case he had ever had anything to do with'.[28]

Where Henry Hayler disappeared to we do not know. He may have gone to Brussels or Paris, as did other pornographers, who, after being hounded out of London, set up operations in Belgium and France.

There was a developing international trade in indecent or obscene photographs. Photographers in Paris who submitted their photographs for official inspection often found them approved 'For Export Only'. This overseas trade relied on the new international postal systems, which then raised fears about the control of and access to questionable material – just as new distribution systems like the Internet prompt concern today. We can get an idea of how this overseas trade might have operated from the case of a certain Walter McIntosh of the Fine-Art Photographers' Publishing Co. of 20 Rathbone Place, off Oxford Street, London. McIntosh dealt in photographs of fine art from the Paris salons, famous historical paintings and landscapes; he also distributed photographs of animals – wild and domestic; in addition he had a line in 'Artists' Female Models, photographed direct from life – artistic poses, nude and semi-nude'. In 1894 he was sending letters to the notorious dealer Adolf Estinger in Budapest, requesting miniatures from what he referred to as the 'X' collection and requiring that they be sent to a separate name and address 'in double strong envelopes well sealed'. At the same time he was sending out unsolicited circulars to 'enlightened persons of culture, education and responsibility' in the United States to expand his sales in nudes and semi-nudes. This in fact was to be his undoing, as one of the persons of culture, education and responsibility – a George A. Guernsey Esq. – complained to the Postmaster General of the United States, who in turn complained to the Postmaster General of England.[29]

Photography, like print before it, was a great mechanical invention. It allowed identical images to be struck again and again – in their thousands – at minimal cost. Even more than print, it was a democratizing medium; a popular medium in the broadest sense. Ordinary people could produce, control, distribute and purchase the photograph. Images were immediate and accessible, and did not depend on literacy. The photograph, unlike the painting, was not tied to a small community of artists, patrons and critics who 'fixed' the sexual image in codes of social acceptability. This was the democratization of pornography.

Dirty pictures were produced in their thousands, bought and sold in urban centres and trafficked in and around Europe. Scurrilous nudes and shocking images decorated open display cases and populated locked backroom cupboards for customers with specialized tastes. Scandalous stereographs titillated the drawing rooms of the privileged and Victorian gentlemen's toys ingeniously concealed racy photographs. Pedlars made a living by touting their obscene images around the European cities; ordinary people – husbands and wives like M. and Mme Lamarre – ran profitable sidelines to their petit bourgeois family concerns; established photographic studios swelled their profits while protecting themselves from official disapproval by the covert use of middlemen.

In short, the trade in dirty pictures was alive and kicking in the nineteenth century, and it was an important part of the new world of photography. Yet in one of those episodes that underlines the equivocal nature of 'history' – history as it happened compared to history as it is written – the early pornographic photograph has simply dropped out of sight. Numerous books on photography barely touch on it, or perhaps, more accurately, avert their gaze. Our collective photographic memories are well populated with early landscapes, urban settings, family portraits and portraits of the rich, famous, literary and eccentric. It is Julia Margaret Cameron's 'Thomas Carlyle' (1867), Henry Peach Robinson's 'Fading Away' (1858), Alexander Gardner's 'Scouts and Guides to the Army of the Potomac' (1862) that frame our ideas of early photography. But photographic nudes that produced income and technical knowledge, and forged distribution channels and trade links in the new dynamic photographic industry are nowhere to be seen. They were certainly both seen and commented upon in the nineteenth century, yet they have disappeared from view in the twentieth.

The result of this is to distort not only the history of photography but also the era that invented it. If it is only the tasteful nude daguerreotype that is permitted to surface from the nineteenth century, we recast the age as 'repressed but saucy'. And such selectivity both misreads the nineteenth century and threatens to misrepresent the present. Contrary to popular belief, it did not take the 1960s and the Internet to create the phenomenon of hard-core. What we would call hard-core today was there right from the beginning: beaver shots, fellatio, cunnilingus, girl on girl, boy on boy, threesomes, orgies, golden showers, flagellation …

As Abigail Solomon-Godeau says:

> …all the conventions of pose and body display we are familiar with from contemporary imagery – the beaver shot, the masturbating woman – appear fully formed, as it were, in its [photography's] earliest incarnations. It is as if these ritual displays are invented *for* the camera, in relation to its technical abilities and technical deficiencies.[30]

△ Daguerreotype, anonymous, c.1855.

As Professor Linda Williams from the University of California, who is in the frontline of academic research into pornography, remarks, 'It's funny, when I teach pornography, my students are so shocked that the conventions that are used today, like the direct bold stare, and the sexual positions that they think are so modern, go all the way back to antiquity.'[31]

The reproducibility of the photograph and its relative cheapness created significant opportunities for wide-ranging public access to such images. Even the most classical or artistic of nudes, however, were vulnerable to police and court action at a time of considerable confusion over obscenity legislation and practice. Through the nineteenth and twentieth centuries, however, the principal battles over obscenity were waged not over photography but over literature. These battles were fought on an increasingly sophisticated defence: that the literary work had artistic merit. This also had an impact on photography. Nudity was not to be portrayed for its own sake. In order to avoid the label 'obscene', it had to be redeemed by a more ennobling institution – art or knowledge. This is just like, and is in fact related to, the Christian injunction that sex was not to be enjoyed for its own sake, but needed to be redeemed by a more ennobling institution – in this case marriage. Once again, the treatment of sexual imagery takes its cue from the status of sex. Sex and sexual representation threatened to be obscene; with no redemption they were absolutely obscene – a quasi-legal elaboration that echoes our Christian heritage.

If this kind of approach led to a discernible hypocrisy in sexual matters, the same was true with the publication of naked images. Using the framework of art studies to justify the publication of photographs, 'art' magazines were bought by non-artists and the magazines avoided censure. And often where a more general magazine chose to publish such photographs, the layouts were accompanied by rousing editorials. For instance, when the American *Metropolitan Magazine* published nude models posed as reproductions of 'classical' art in 1895, it felt the need to justify this in a homily to the purity of classical studies of the nude, commenting, 'The older civilizations of the world

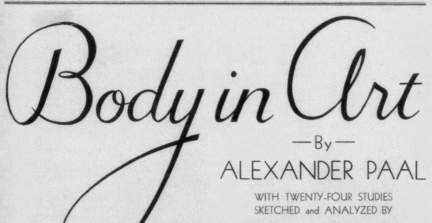

Body in Art

—By—

ALEXANDER PAAL

WITH TWENTY-FOUR STUDIES
SKETCHED and ANALYZED BY

ARTHUR ZAIDENBERG
INSTRUCTOR IN DRAWING

SEVENTY-THREE LIFE SIZE NUDES

Body In Art is primarily intended as a book for the art student and teacher. The models have been selected, the poses arranged, for the satisfaction of searchers after art instruction. It is to satisfy their desires, their hopes, their ambitions that this truly magnificent gallery of body studies has been collected. It is to awaken and sharpen their artistic abilities that simple, easily followed, step-by-step instruction in sketching has been provided.

In the long history of arts; starting with the Renaissance in Europe; every artist was first thoroughly grounded by a study of the human nude figure. In other words, the foundation of all art study has forever been to sketch from the living model; posing in the beauty of the God-created body.

Also as the history of art proves, it is the feminine figure that has been the chief study of artists. The reason for this is quite obvious. The variety and variation of curves in a woman's body are far more interesting and inviting to the sense of the esthetic than is true of the male figure.

$4.00 per copy

Delivered to your address from

HEALTH PUBLICATIONS PUBLISHING CO.
172 John St.   -   -   Toronto 2B, Ont.

◁ *Body in Art*, Toronto, May 1946. Magazines and books featuring photographs of naked women often found a wider readership than their editorials claimed to seek. This introduction reads, '*Body in Art* is primarily intended as a book for the art student and teacher. The models have been selected, the poses arranged, for the satisfaction of searchers after art instruction...The variety and variation of curves in a woman's body are far more interesting and inviting to the sense of the aesthetic than is true of the male figure.'

have long since decided that only prurient and bestial minds see suggestion and wickedness in classical studies of the nude.'[32] Magazines that claimed to be an invaluable tool for serious photographers and artists had oddly bad photographs, and, equally, magazines supposedly advocating the philosophy of nudism or naturalism would have disproportionate numbers of photographs of young women. (As with the supposed *académies* in Paris that preceded them, demand indicated a level unlikely to be matched by a genuine interest in naturalism.)

The other route was to publish images that were just the right side of the law in terms of exposed flesh, while unabashedly exploiting the 'sex appeal'. (This was a genre that demonstrated with considerable clarity the 'coded' nature of the photograph, for if

RED HAIRED, VIVACIOUS, INDOOR TYPE

Lauri Del Mar poses, primps, paints and practices prettily for the HIT SHOW enthusiasts. She is currently at the Silver Slipper in Las Vegas, Nev.

Battle of the *Bosoms!*

Winnie Garrett, the Riotous Red-head, boasts a 39" bust! How many movie stars can match that, boys?

Tempest Storm, the torrid tornado from out West, measures a terrific 43" at the bust, and she dares any movie queen to beat that!

Evelyn West, famous peeler, had her bust insured for $50,000 by Lloyds!

△ (Left) The 1940s were captivated by legs, whereas the 1950s (right) focused on women's breasts.

▷ (Top) The 1960s brought us the bottom, and (below) the 1970s revealed pubic hair for the first time (*Penthouse*, centrefold, June 1972).

the uniqueness of the photograph was its referential quality, its 'trace of the real', what it shared with every other representation was that the image was coded.) 'Girlie magazines' and 'men's magazines', which had their first incarnations in the fan magazines featuring the smiling and then pouting Hollywood stars, were part of a genre that did not really come into its own until the 1940s. From then on the magazines progressed decade by decade from the tame to the explicit: the 1940s gave us legs, the 1950s gave us breasts, the 1960s gave us bottoms and the 1970s gave us the crotch.[33]

In the 1970s the 'pink wars', as they became known in the trade, saw a battle over the crotch: first it was pubic hair, then it was the genitals, then it was the spread vulva. Or, in the words of the magazines, first it was bush, then it was beaver, then it was split beaver. What started with the first glimpses of pubic hair in *Penthouse* was pushed to its gynaecological limits by the new magazine of raunch, Larry Flynt's *Hustler*, in the latter half of the 1970s.

The desire to see female genitalia close up had been part of the pornographic repertoire for centuries, yet it was photography that put this voyeuristic impulse centre stage. There is something about the camera that makes it peculiarly suited to this aspect of pornography. The camera brings with it possibilities of fragmentation. As one outraged observer was to note in 1861, 'People not only sell obscene photographs – they do better than that. They sell them with a magnifying glass whereby you can search for microscopic details.'[34] Unlike paintings, drawings and prints, where the image is taken as

a whole and closer inspection of the parts will yield nothing but meaningless lines, the photograph seemed able to yield more information on closer inspection of its parts. Increasingly sophisticated lenses and enlargers superseded the magnifying glass, of course, and the 'close-up' would become a defining feature of photography.

According to Abigail Solomon-Godeau, the new technology of the camera represents a radical break with the technologies of the past and produces its own pornography: 'The "beaver" shot seems not to have pre-existed photography. Before photography sex was understood as an activity. It's something one, two, three, or ten people do together. But what one sees in photography is the beaver, a part of the body, decontextualized. It is about a radical fragmenting of the body that seems to have no predecessor in, say, lithographic pornography. The shift is from sexuality as an activity to sexuality as a forbidden sight.'[35]

The 'pink wars' of the mainstream quality men's magazines in the 1970s are an example of the technology determining its own market: the camera fuelled the desire to see more and more. This was the 'frenzy of the visible' in the mainstream soft-core market; each step broke the next barrier to intimacy, the next barrier to seeing.

Mark Gabor, author of *The Pin Up: A Modest History* and *An*

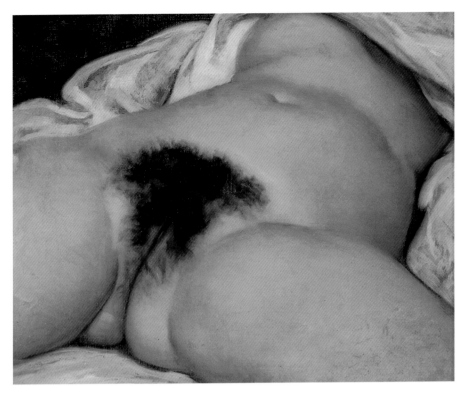

Illustrated History of Girlie Magazines ('I think the name that fits the genre most appropriately is "girlie magazine", because it's basically about exploiting women, and to call a woman a "girlie" is like calling a black man "boy"'), says, 'It was the readiness of the readership. Publishers found that they could, as time went on, release hotter and hotter pictures and readers were ready for it. Some magazines went too far for their steady readership and folded. So you had to maintain this very delicate line, and the success of any men's magazine was in their ability to know exactly the line to which they could walk – up to the line, but not across the line – that would keep their readership interested and always moving progressively forward to more and more boldness. *Penthouse*, really from the time it started, was the innovator in this.'[36]

In a landmark edition of *Penthouse* in April 1970, the magazine took the radical step of showing pubic hair in its centrefold. The founder of *Penthouse*, Bob Guccione, recalls, 'In those days if you showed pubic hair, you stepped over the boundary and you were producing pornography or obscene material. So we took that very big and very dramatic step – I could have gone to jail if things turned out the wrong way. And we continued to push the envelope. Today *Penthouse* is completely explicit. It's totally X-rated. We even introduced the first pictures of women peeing and no one's ever seen this before except in very specialized, fetish

PENTHOUSE FORUM

Peeing for Pleasure

Recently our local watering hole held its first amateur Piss Off night. And what a pisser it was. Even though I had never done anything like it before, I made sure I was first in line to jump in and get my feet wet!

will select the best ones, based on graphic excellence, volume, stream, trajectory, distance, and erotic appeal. Winners' pictures may be published in our magazines and/or on our Websites, and you'll be paid at our special rates for this promotion. Full details will

Penthouse permission to publish them. Unfortunately, photos cannot be returned.—The Editors.

Pees on Earth

I would like to congratulate Penthouse for choosing Jasmine Raff to bring in the new year in your January 1999 issue. Jasmine's firm, round ass and succulent shaved pink pussy turned me on big-time. Her photos are a piss lover's dream come true. Seeing her natural juices streaming out of her luscious lips got my cock fully erect. Jasmine can do 'what comes naturally' for me anytime, anywhere.

It would be great if you could publish a Best of The Great American 'Pissing Contest' issue. In the meantime, keep the pictures flowing. You've made a faithful peevert out of me!—B.M., New Jersey

Shot by Shot

A peeing video? Oh, my goodness. Penthouse, urine the money now—or could be. You say there are no plans for such a video at this time, but let's hope the idea doesn't get shelved permanently.

magazines devoted entirely to that subject. We got a letter from a woman who said, have you ever seen anything like this? And she sent us a Polaroid of herself peeing. And I thought – just for the hell of it – I'm going to publish it, because we're, you know, we're always looking for something new. So this became a big feature. We're now running the great American pissing contest under the title of "Pissing Off America".[37]

Peeing for the camera, however, was not new. It is there right from the beginning, in nineteenth-century photographs, and indeed follows a pre-photographic interest in the chamberpot. The mainstream magazines were reinventing the wheel and calling it a 'sexual revolution'.

What photographs and then the photo magazines gave was control and privacy. They provided detailed realism, sexual poses and fantasy combinations in a medium that required no additional equipment, like video machines or film projectors; they can be carried with you or hidden away. Sometimes called 'one-handed magazines', they do the job. As Mark Gabor says, 'Whether it's just for looking or for something like masturbation, the man has total control of the magazine. He can switch from pose to pose or model to model by the mere flipping of a page. He gets his control over the image, which is basically over the woman, which is what his fantasy is all about, which is manipulation and objectification of the woman.'[38]

But within a few decades of its invention, photography was upstaged by its progeny, as the pornographic urge for more – to see more, to have more action, to know more – was fulfilled by a new medium: the moving image.

△ (Top left) 'Pissing off America' on the letters page of *Penthouse*, April 1999. (Top right) Daguerreotype, *c*.1855, anonymous. (Bottom) Seventeenth-century engraving, *The Piss-pot*, anonymous.

Twentieth Century Foxy

The screening of *The Kiss* (1896), one of the earliest-known film sequences, prompted the Chicago publisher Herbert S. Stone to complain, 'The prolonged pasturing on each other's lips was hard to bear . . . magnified to Gargantuan proportions and repeated three times over it is absolutely disgusting.'[1] He demanded the intervention of the police.

Whatever photography offered, film seemed to promise more. If photography offered a new visual erotic, film could outstrip it, catching not only one but many moments. In addition, the sequential moments, moments across time, brought with them a different kind of visual experience: the pleasure of seeing bodies in movement.

△ *The Kiss* (1896).

◁ *Peeping Tom* (1960). A story of psychopathology, sex and death; the camera itself features centrally in the story as an instrument of voyeurism.

The photographic image was never just about seeing; it was also about knowing. The camera was what French film scholar Jean Louis Comolli has called a 'machine of the visible', and it was seen as a tool of measurement right from the start, a tool of science as much as a tool of art. This combined promise of seeing more and knowing more is demonstrated in the pioneering work of Eadweard Muybridge. One Leland Stanford, a former governor of California and horse breeder, bet that, contrary to the belief of his contemporaries, there was a point at which all four hooves of a horse leave the ground in a fast trot. And to settle the question he brought in Muybridge in 1873 to capture the trot of his favourite horse with his so-called 'instantaneous photography'. Sure enough, there in

the sequential photographs was the visual evidence that proved him right. The camera had seen what the eye could not.

Instantaneous photographs were soon being used to capture short sequences of movement as men and women (in various stages of undress) performed tasks like walking, leaping and running. Then there are the photographic records from the clinic of renowned French neurologist Charcot, at the Salpêtrière in Paris, showing women in the grip of 'hysterical' convulsions. These photographs demonstrate a kind of visual hunger under the guise of scientific study: a combined desire for knowledge and voyeurism, what Professor Linda Williams at the University of California has called 'scientism and prurience.'[2]

The camera is an instrument to reveal and examine in detail what is otherwise not easily seen. One of the earliest films is Fred Ott's *Sneeze*, an Edison Laboratory test film (1893–4). This was first published as a series of photos in an article that enthuses about the 'partially unseen'[3] being revealed for the first time by the kinetoscope images.

From the beginning, then, film was attempting to see more of what was hidden – to look behind and discover what was normally out of view. It appealed to the perverse tendency to value knowledge that is hidden from us more than knowledge that is easily available.

So, film is a medium that promises to see more and know more. And extremism is implicit here, because there is always more to see, more to know. This is a compulsion of the medium; there is a tendency to maximum visibility. It is no coincidence that the first films showed human operations in full detail, real-life executions from around the world, the electrocution of an elephant, animals attacking other animals, two lions killing an elephant and even in one instance a film-maker who forced a horse over a cliff to capture its dramatic and bloody end.

The film camera, then, would inevitably focus its voracious and greedy eye on sex

▷ Eadweard Muybridge's sequences of so-called 'instantaneous photography' (*c.*1880) embodied film's twin impulses to know more and see more.

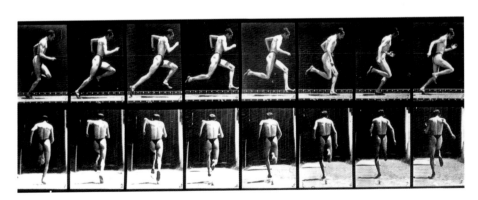

and the body. Sex and film were bound to come together. The naked body, the genitals, the act of sex – these were all things that were normally hidden. And predictably, from the start, films attempted to explore what was not available to be seen. And, as Williams points out, this exploration is sometimes expressly acknowledged in titles like *Wonders of the Unseen World* and *Pull Down the Curtain, Susie.*[4]

'A new kind of eye has been turned on the world and immediately what does it want to see, it wants to see the woman blinking at you, it wants to see the woman taking off her clothes. There are many forms of pornography, but film is a natural medium for pornography,' says Linda Williams.[5]

Film, like photography, offered the pleasure of seeing without the responsibility of looking. While voyeurism is embedded in the tradition of Western art – as John Berger has said, 'Men look at women. Women watch themselves being looked at'[6] – the filmic image introduced a whole different dimension. The ability of the camera to act as a surrogate eye had no equal. What else could give such an uninterrupted view of the real person without being seen itself? The voyeur, after all, wants to see, but does not want to be seen. Photography allowed the visual pleasure of seeing real women, real sex, without being seen.

Behind the filmic image, however, lies an illusion. The trace of the real encourages hopeless quests and offers beguiling promises of truth and knowledge. Of course, like photography, what is filmed is no longer there, for film only records a series of single moments: you are not being offered the real thing, but only the trace of it from moments now gone. There is an ultimate frustration here, a sense of absence and of loss.

It is often remarked that pornography too promises what it cannot deliver; that it arouses desire for the object which cannot be satisfied and so is essentially fraudulent. And some people see in this the frustration and melancholy that stigmatize pornography: the lone male in the dirty raincoat who is unable or unwilling to engage in real relationships. In this view, the consumption of pornography is nothing but a failure to make genuine social connections.

For the authorities and the upper echelons of society, however, it was not what film failed to deliver that weighed on them, but rather what it succeeded in delivering. This was a question of class from the beginning. Thomas Edison's kinetoscope (the viewing apparatus created in 1891 to project the images of the kinetograph, the early motion-picture camera), was almost immediately turned into peepshow machines. Arcades everywhere promised a glimpse of 'What the Butler Saw' (although in reality what the butler saw was very little indeed). And the fears expressed by moral reformers, local bigwigs and self-appointed guardians of society betrayed class distaste and class anxiety.

△ Muybridge showed his photographic sequences on a 'zoopraxiscope', a kind of magic lantern that worked as an early projector. So life-like was the result that, in one case, a dog barked and ran after the images of the horses on the screen.

Rather than what was seen, it was who was doing the seeing – eyes glued to the 'peepers', unhealthily excited by the prospect of access to the forbidden. Or, even more disturbing, those same excitable lower-class eyes glued to the flickering images on the walls of dark converted shops that smelled of urinals, the 'pennygaffs'.

Film brought a new organization of the senses, a new 'frenzy of the visible'[7], and this in turn threatened to engage some deep atavistic responses. In 1913 one commentator remarked:

> It is not merely harmless fascination with moving images and colour, but a terrifying lust, as powerful and violent as the deepest passions. It's the kind of rush that makes the blood boil and the head spin until that bafflingly potent excitement, common to every passion, races through the flesh . . .
>
> This ghastly pleasure in seeing atrocities, violence and death lies dormant in us all. It is this kind of pleasure which brings us, hurrying, to the morgue, to the scene of the crime, to every chase, to every street fight, and makes us pay good money for a glimpse of sodomy. And this is what draws the masses into the cinemas as if they were possessed. Cinema offers the masses the kind of pleasure which, day by day, is eroded by the advance of civilization.[8]

▷ *Extase* (1933) became notorious for featuring not only the nudity of Hedy Lamarr, but also a close-up of her face during orgasm.

If these 'pleasures' could be eroded by the advance of civilization, the medium that promoted them must threaten not only to halt civilization but even to reverse it.

Film is a medium that moves. The sprocketed celluloid moves through the gate, the sequential projected images give the illusion of movement and the identification with real bodies in action has the ability to move the viewer. Sometimes literally. When the Lumière brothers first showed their films of an oncoming train, people literally jumped out of their seats to make their escape, so lifelike was the image. Films make you cry, scare you, arouse you. This visceral potential of film was recognized from the beginning, and with that recognition came deep suspicion of the potential social impact of the new medium.

In the Victorian era, there had been much anxiety about anything that threatened to 'move' people. There was a fear of the kinetic experience, of movement within the spectator, of anything that might disturb sensibilities. The spectre of revolution still stalked Europe and the potential of the uncontrolled masses raised fears, if not always articulated, about social disorder, as well as more mundane concerns about retaining an effective and productive workforce in an industrial age. Film was a medium that threatened to engage the lower emotions of those most vulnerable, or least able to control themselves – women, children and the uneducated.

As was true for those watching the Lumière train, the terrifying immediacy of larger-than-life screen images engendered a panic – this time a social and moral one. In Europe and America, steps were taken to control the new medium. In March 1902 the People's Institute of New York established the National Board of Censorship as a film review board, and later the film industry instituted a form of voluntary self-regulation through the Motion Picture Producers Association and its 1930 Hays Code. Censorship was established in Germany in 1908 and in Sweden in 1911. Britain had its

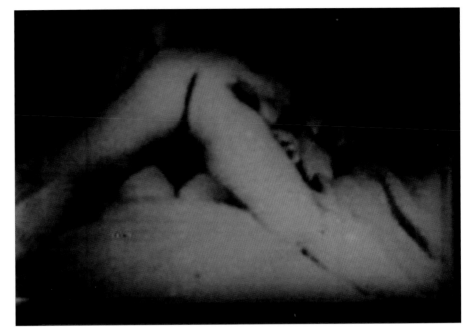

▷ *College Co-ed* (*1953*). A popular camera angle in the 'stag' or 'blue movie': the film medium, in its restless search to know more and see more, favoured angles that were normally hidden from the view even of the participants.

Cinematograph Act in 1909 and its British Board of Film Censors in 1913, while the National Council for Public Morals conducted hasty fact-finding missions in 1917 and judges declared the cinematograph shows 'a grave danger to the community'. As well as betraying their class disdain for the vulgar new medium, these voices are evidence of the widely held belief that proletarian audiences were particularly susceptible to disruptive influences. In fact, for these critics film's only virtue appeared to be that while it was being watched the working classes were not drinking. Film would be the most censored medium until the introduction of television, which would take on film's mantle as the new mass medium or, more to the point, the new medium of the masses.

The anxiety about the potential of film to move audiences encompassed a number of genres. Horror, for instance, faced the constraints of a censorship system keen to minimize the visceral impact and imbue the new medium with a restrained, moderate and cerebral aesthetic. Films now considered classics were problematic at the time: *Nosferatu* (1922) was banned by the British Board of Film Censors and *The Cabinet of Dr Caligari* (1919) was heavily cut before it could be released.

Just as film got going, so too did the censorship system. When the British Board of Film Censorship came into being in 1913, it had only two specific rules: no materialization of Christ and no nudity. This put paid to sex and nudity in the public cinema for decades to come. But rather than ridding the world of depictions of sex in film, the censorship system created a dramatically polarized film output. While the viewing fare of mainstream audiences was rigorously controlled, highly explicit films were playing in 'smoking rooms' and brothels. As these were not publicly exhibited, they were not subject to censorship rules. In the London smoking rooms, there is no record of confiscation of such films during the Edwardian era; rather, there was a *de facto* tolerance by the police.

Rarely clear cut, censorship tends to function to restrict or privilege some audiences over others. As Laurence O'Toole says, 'People mistakenly think censorship is an absolute issue. You either can see something or you're stopped from seeing something. More often than not, it is murkier and muddier than that. Maybe you get to see things, but it's going to be hard finding them, and you may have to take a few risks – you might have to go to certain areas of town which are seedy and not too welcoming. So only a certain number of people are going to go, gain access to these materials. That is why pornography in the UK has been quite sexist, because the point of sale has been a fairly male-orientated domain, and the restrictions on what can be shown mean that there is less for the female heterosexual viewer than there is for the male viewer.'[9]

In these smoking rooms and brothels, we can see again the mechanism of the secret museum, where material was accessible to some sections while others – women and children – were locked out. And the twin tracks of publicly available, censored material and privately circulated, non-censored material continued until the 1970s, when, for a brief spell, it looked as if hard-core might merge with the mainstream.

In the meantime, early sexually explicit films – 'stag films' or 'blue movies' – were in their own solitary slipstream – or, more accurately perhaps, their own stagnant pool. One of the more remarkable features about stag films is that they barely changed over the decades, remaining relatively low quality, single reel, black and white and (long after the introduction of 'talkies') silent. They endlessly repeated the same formula – meeting of protagonists, foreplay, penetration ('the meat shot'), end of film. Over and over again. Stag was primitive and pockmarked by its technical limitations. While mainstream cinema went from technical strength to strength, inventing creative new narrative strategies along the way, the one-reeler stag film remained mired in technical underachievement and radical narrative discontinuities. Why? Not because it couldn't but because it didn't need to; it was already delivering. Illegally shot, illegally distributed, illegally consumed, it already gave what was wanted: that which you could not get elsewhere. The stag staged – mainstream did not – a genital show. And what was important was not just the visual show, but the knowledge that it was real – real people, real sex. This is not the arena of mainstream 'make-believe', with its suspension of disbelief; people were actually having sex and you could see them doing it.

Although some years later, Alex deRenzy, one of the most successful porn directors, discovered the same lesson: 'We were getting a little artistic, we were getting artistic with our smut. And I had this customer who comes out and he says, "deRenzy," and I say, "Yeah?" He says, "Don't forget the point. Don't forget the point." And boy, I've carried that in my head ever since. Whenever I go to make a movie, I sit down: "Boy, remember

△ *College Co-ed.* As the century progressed the 'blue movie' did not. In distinction to the increasing sophistication of mainstream cinema, the blue movie became mired in technical and narrative deficiencies.

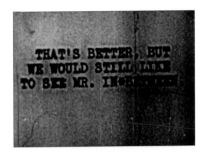

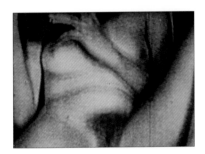

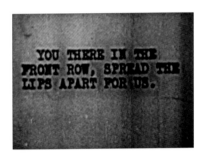

△ *The Virgin With the Hot Pants* (c.1923–1925). The film is a disjointed collection of unconnected scenes and the inter-titles display a common feature of the early blue movies: the pervasive sense of Us and Them.

the point. What is the point?" And so if I get a choice between something real sticky or a little art, I'll put the sticky in every time.'[10]

What was the point of stag? The answer is not in the content alone, as an account in *Die Schaubühne* of an early stag film in Berlin by Kurt Tucholsky shows:

Nobody spoke out loud, since everyone was a bit anxious; they only murmured. The screen turned white; a fragile, mottled silver-white light appeared, trembling. It began. But everyone laughed, myself included. We had expected something bizarre and extravagent. We saw a meow-kitty and a woof-doggy romping on the screen. Maybe the exporter had tacked the scene on to fool the police – who knows? The film ran without music, rattling monotonously; it was gloomy and not very pleasant . . .

Things remained *gemütlich* in the cinema. We didn't realize that even *Tristan and Isolde* would seem ridiculous in this setting . . .

The only reason [the patrons] didn't play cards was because it was too dark. An atmosphere of healthy and hearty pleasure prevailed. The ending was too obscure, so that when it was over everyone thought there was more to come – it just goes to show, that's how it is with sex. The men stood around feeling self-conscious and embarrassed, remarking on the lack of values here and in general. And then we pushed through narrow passageways into an adjoining establishment where the music was loud and shrill, and everyone was strangely quiet and excited. I heard later that the proprietor had ordered twenty call girls.[11]

This seems to have been an uncomfortable experience. In a public place the voyeur can be seen. Here there was the embarrassed air of having been caught masturbating, if only figuratively, in public. The privacy that would later be afforded by video and the Internet was absent. Instead individuals in the audience were pushed back into their public and social personas: 'The men stood around feeling self-conscious . . .' But if later media would replace these discomforts with unimpeded voyeurism, they would also lose something. For stag delivered what the new media could not: a male-only social ritual.

Here the male spectator is not merely presumed, but actual. The stags were addressed to men, quite literally, as certain inter-titles make clear. In one film, *The Virgin with the Hot Pants* (1923), a card addresses a member of the audience: 'You there in the front row, spread the lips apart for us.' This is followed by a close-up of a pair of male hands spreading apart a woman's labia. And again, this time to the woman in the film: 'Turn over, honey, so that we can see how it looks from behind', which she obligingly does, displaying her genitals to the camera. It is the language of Us and Them. The films often incorporate dirty jokes and employ a transgressive, often adolescent male humour. One early film has credits that read: 'Seduced by A. Prick, Directed by Ima Cunt, Photographed by R. U. Hard.' And in *The Plumber Does a Little Plumbing* the screen captions were in limerick form:

> The name of our plumber is Lee,
> The girl in the story's Marie.
> She said, 'Stop your plumbing,
> I hear someone coming!'
> Said Lee, 'No one's coming but me!'

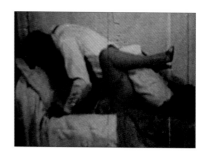

The lines exhibited a casual and jokey machismo. In the 1930s the film *A Stiff Game* has a caption explaining that Sambo 'collects heavy on some white meat and hair pie' prior to a scene of cunnilingus.[12] Their collective viewing no doubt provided the occasion to enact a shared and socially sanctioned masculine identity in a process of male acculturation. Women were locked out. Stags were made by and for men. They were rarely sadistic, but frequently misogynistic. They are textbook examples of the sexual objectification of women, where women function only as objects of interest, their subjectivity acknowledged only if it advances spurious and flimsy plot-lines.

The pornographic world of stag is a world of sexual plenty. Women are compliant, men dominant. It is a world full of easy sexual opportunities without consequence or responsibility. Sex can happen at any time, anywhere, and, of course, it always does. We are in the world of what Steven Marcus has called 'pornotopia', a never-never world where 'time and space measure nothing but sexual encounters'. Marcus is talking about literature but his ideas are equally applicable to film. As he says:

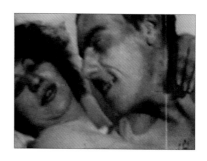

△ *A Country Stud-Horse.* The pornographic world of stag is one of sexual plenty where women are compliant and men dominant.

> To the question, 'What time is it in pornotopia?' one is tempted to answer, 'It is always bedtime' . . . All men in it are always and infinitely potent; all women fecundate with lust and flow inexhaustibly with sap or juice or both. Everyone is always ready for anything, and everyone is infinitely generous with his substance.[13]

Early stag seems awkward and clumsy to the modern eye. Cameras, also awkward and clumsy, are planted for a big wide shot where the action takes place. Protagonists often come in and out of this shot as if the screen were a stage. And, like a live performance on a stage, you get only one shot at it. Couplings may be unsuccessful, unconvincing and uninspired: interest flags, jollity breaks out, penises droop. Early stag shows little interest in passion or excitement, or even pleasure. There is also a promiscuity of sexual identity: a man will penetrate a woman, then be penetrated by a man and then penetrate another man with a casualness that underlines the modernity of concepts of 'homosexual' (first used in 1897) and even, for that matter, 'sexuality' (first used, in 1800). What was important to stag was the transgressive

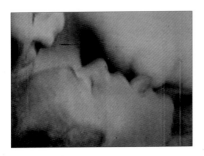

△ *Smart Aleck* was *the*
blue movie of the 1950s
and its star, Candy Barr,
became an underground
celebrity.

sexual act.

Another striking feature is the breakdown in narrative coherence. There is usually a consistent story built around some kind of encounter – nun meets monk in the garden/man picks up two women in car/man surprises woman masturbating – but when it comes to the actual sex the storyline breaks down, with unexplained couplings followed by misplaced close-ups followed by radical time-shifts. In the era that predated both the zoom lens and camera portability, the lack of continuity between wide shots and medium shots and close-ups can be seen as a technical limitation. But this is not simply a technical question. Even when equipment improved, these discontinuities remained a feature of the blue movie. Everything leads up to the act of penetration, which then overwhelms all other considerations of meaningfulness and consistency. The lip-service paid to film conventions is abandoned to a visual frenzy of repeated couplings. As Linda Williams points out, this is a characteristic that goes back to the very earliest cinema, in which 'fascination with cinematic movement for movement's sake was paramount'.[14]

Like photography, the medium immediately explored everything there was to see: explicit shots of penetration (in early American stag, the recurrent motif was the low-angle shot between the legs – an angle not available to the participants – to reveal penetration in the missionary position), fellatio, cunnilingus and bestiality. In one early film, a smiling woman is shown bringing in a dog that proceeds to lick her between the legs and then, in a series of rather disjointed and non-consecutive images, mount her.

While material like this was circulating illegally, the policies of the censorship boards had a stranglehold on what could be shown in mainstream cinema. Even 'moral' films or those designed to give public information easily fell foul of the censor. *Damaged Goods* (1919), which was responding to concerns about returning servicemen with VD and tells the story of a man who contracts the disease after a single night with a prostitute, was refused a certificate. There were no explicit scenes; it was the subject matter itself that was offensive. In Belfast, however, the authorities decided that the film could be exhibited on condition that it was shown to segregated audiences, with men down one side of the aisle and women on the other.[15] Again we see the potent mix of the fear of sexual representation and the fear that it might in some way adversely arouse the masses. While the blue movies were cracking jokes about meat and hair pies, expressions like 'bottom's up Auntie' and 'Tonight's the night' were edited out of mainstream films in the UK. And in America, while the stag films were filming up close and personal, in the 1930s the Hays Office was issuing guidelines like 'No inside thigh of a female may be shown between the garter and the knickers' and 'If two people are shown on a bed, they must have at least one foot on the floor', and words like 'virgin' were banned.

As the century progressed, the blue movie did not. But just as film pornography was becoming totally predictable, its future took an unexpected turn and the world of the blue movie went public.

The most significant blue movie of the 1950s was *Smart Aleck*, starring Juanita Slushes a.k.a. Candy Barr, who was the undisputed porn queen of the blue-movie circuit. As Laurence O'Toole says, 'She was simultaneously famous and unheard of: a popular secret, known and lusted over by countless viewers in confidence, truly the cult celebrity.'[16] This was still a time when obtaining pornographic films was fraught with the uncertainties of any illegal activity; the production of blue movies was what Al Di Lauro and Gerald Rabkin describe as a 'haphazard, high-risk, low-profit, regional activity . . . the stag was, in essence, a cottage industry'.[17] Even with the new 8mm black and white loops, which allowed small-scale production and greater access and possibilities for domestic use, the viewing of pornographic material was fraught with uncertainty. As O'Toole points out, you had to risk a red-light area, or buy the right magazines with the right adverts and hope that the suppliers were genuine. There was little comeback: the dissatisfied customer was as likely to take his complaint to the police as the police were to take him seriously.

At the beginning of the new decade, there was no reason to think the 1960s would be much different. Sex in society at large had not been invented yet. In *A Kind of Loving* (1962) a young man (played by Alan Bates) enters a chemist's to buy contraceptives, only to emerge with a bottle of Lucozade. The situation was not only instantly recognizable, it was emblematic of a society that was profoundly, if comically, uncomfortable about sex. And as if to underline the same point, the British Board of Film Censors had great problems with the scene at script stage. According to the director, John Schlesinger, 'The censor's advance view was that, if the mention of contraceptives was allowed here in an admittedly legitimate context, it weakened the position of opposing it in some other context where it might be exploited.'[18] Schlesinger prevailed on this particular occasion, but this was an age when the censor could require actress Leslie Caron to cover her nipples with Elastoplast for a nude scene in the *L-Shaped Room*

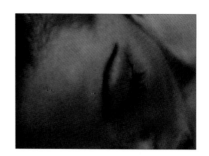

(1962) and off-screen references to abortions had to be cut altogether, while words like 'bugger' were changed to 'begger' in *Saturday Night, Sunday Morning* (1960). In vetting the script prior to filming, the British censor John Trevelyan informed producer Harry Saltzman:

△ *Arcade*, from the 1960s, gives a different angle on fellatio when the male protagonist turns out to be the cameraman.

The love scenes can be passionate but should not go too far. The director should use discretion in shooting them. The line 'Get down in bed' is perhaps rather direct . . . As I said in my earlier letter, we would prefer the phrase 'knocking on

△ *I am Curious Yellow*
(1967), created a furore
when it was released, and
created fears that 'stag'
was breaking through into
the mainstream.

wi' a married woman' to be altered. Would not 'mucking about wi' a married woman' be equally good here?

The 1960s soon produced a wave of youthful and sexual rebellions that made these obsessive, nuanced acts of censorship look rather hopeless: miniskirts, the Beatles, the Stones, the Pill, 'free love' – this was the new 'permissive society'. But Canute-like the BBFC persisted against the tide of new experimentation – particularly experimentation from the Continent. When the film *I am Curious Yellow* (1967), directed by Vilgot Sjoman, was released in Sweden the advance press was breathless. *Variety* declared, '[it] reaches new explicitness in the depiction of sexual acts', while another newspaper warned, 'On no account should this film be shown in Great Britain . . . It is a danger to every human being', and American and Norwegian authorities found that it was not fit for showing. When it came to the BBFC for certification in Britain, one examiner reported, 'I do not think there is any point in discussing whether this film is "dirty" or not. For most people "dirty" is roughly equivalent to lecherous, and there can be no doubt that this film is inordinately lecherous.' There was deep suspicion at the BBFC that the film was being used as a way of getting the 'stag film' through the front door. One examiner talked of 'specious window-dressing for pornography' and another said, 'There are several suggestions scattered through the film that the director's intention is to get as close to making a "stag movie" as "the censors" will let him . . . I am strongly against the film being given any further attention by the BBFC.' In the event, the film was given a certificate, but only after being heavily cut.

Suddenly there was the spectre of the stag breaking through into the mainstream; the censors' fears of 'specious window-dressing' were being realized. Within a year pornography was legalized in Denmark, and the first film to hit the American cinemas with hard-core material was Alex deRenzy's *Censorship in Denmark: A New Approach* (1969). The 'documentary' format was pornography's Trojan horse. The legal battles over obscenity, largely waged on behalf of literature, allowed for sexually explicit material where there was redeeming social value. The documentary provided an ideal cover: it was not porn, but *about* porn. Such films were texts about pornography rather than pornographic texts; talk about pornography rather than pornographic talk. But not everyone felt the need to justify their pornography. As Lasse Braun, a pornographer and film-maker who has been called the 'Pope of Porn' and the 'Pornographic Anarchist' has said, 'My films are of redeeming social value, against the social damage of censorship.'[19]

In 1967 in San Francisco, Alex deRenzy was already pushing the boundaries of the acceptable: 'there were some arcades in San Francisco and they showed what they called "beaver movies". They show these little beaver movies in between the strippers and these films didn't show anything – maybe a flash of pubic hair of something. And I was shooting news at the time. So I had this soundman and he said let's do one. So we got one of the strippers and we shot one.'

After shooting several more, deRenzy then opened his own place to show his films, which he called the Screening Room: 'We'd show a tiny bit of pubic hair and a little more pubic hair, a little of this, a little of that and every week it was like a frenzy. I mean, the people would line up, what's he gonna do this week? It was really something. It was on the move. At first I felt like I was making dirty little movies and then my brain just went flip all of a sudden one day. I thought that's nothing, it's just a naked girl, we're all adults, what the hell is that? So I just started doing it and that's when I started getting arrested. Got arrested thirty-three times in those three years.'

In the late 1960s Alex deRenzy managed to get hold of *Smart Aleck* for his theatre: 'It was a classic porno movie and every adult male in America had heard about this movie. Well, I came across a copy of it and I said, I've got to show this to my customers. So I put it on the screen and like, Holy Christ, the world caved in. Along came the cops: "You can't do that." And I kept thinking, hey, they're all adults. Of course they can see this movie. And so I showed the movie. We just didn't care any more. To hell with it.'

The blue movie was tolerated when it knew its place. While it apologetically and furtively inhabited its underworld, no one took much notice; it was when it tried to step outside the shadows that the authorities moved in.

Porn had become political again. Rules were being flouted and the authorities were being challenged. This time the revolution went by a different name: the sexual revolution. And as with all revolutions, what was required was a revolutionary vision. To quote Lasse Braun again, 'I remember when Kennedy said that we would go to the moon before the end of the decade, I said to my friends, Come on, if we go to the moon, we have at least to make a little step also in the direction of the liberation of mankind.'

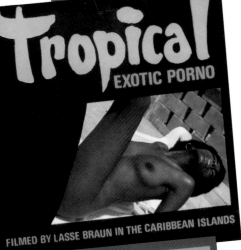

Braun's father was a diplomat and this gave him access to a car with diplomatic number plates. Between 1961 and 1967 he made hundreds of porn runs – with magazines and photos in his boot – shuttling back and forth between Denmark, Spain, Italy, Austria and Belgium. In true revolutionary spirit, he saw it as his mission to convert Europe to his own brand of hedonism; his ambition was to get porn legalizied all over Europe: 'At the time it was forbidden even to show a nude breast, let alone pubic hair. It was totally forbidden everywhere. Nobody knew the meaning of the word "pornography". People would ask me what "pornography" was. If I were caught, it would have become a scandal because of the diplomatic connection. I was distributing a bit everywhere in Europe to create a problem. If you don't have a problem, how could any law-makers take into consideration the legislation of this so-called obscene material? Because legislation was my major goal, I had to provoke something. You know you cannot have a revolution without shocks. And I always considered that I was a revolutionary. I tried to hit people in the stomach, so that they would suddenly realize the extraordinary situation that we were living in with all these laws against sexuality. We should be free.'

Suddenly people were asking what was wrong with nudity, what was wrong with sex. And it wasn't just the men. When Alex deRenzy was filming his little 'beaver

movies', he would simply go up to girls in the street: 'If it hadn't been for the hippie days – '67, '68, '69, – we couldn't have done it. I used to make bets with people. I'd say, I will go round the block and come back with a girl. No, you never. And I'd hop on my bike. You want a job? What doing? I'm making a movie. What kind of movie? A dirty movie – you get naked and roll around a little bit. She'd say OK, how much? I'd say thirty bucks, fifty bucks, whatever the hell it was, and we'd go off and we'd make a movie. I made probably a thousand of them.'

There was a unique combination of sexual insouciance, a desire for experimentation and a frontier mentality that brought ordinary women into experimenting with 'hard-core'. As Georgina Spelvin recalls: 'I was very involved with cinematography as a way to save the world at that point. We were putting together footage of some of the terrible things that were going on in Vietnam and renting cameras and vans and driving down to Washington in order to project these images on public buildings, when someone said that he had a script for a "hard-core" film. I didn't really know what that meant.'[20] Notwithstanding, Spelvin would go on to star in several hard-core films, including the critically acclaimed *Devil in Miss Jones*.

There were new ambitions for sex in film. Having asked whether it needed to be confined to the plotless discontinuities of the stag, people were beginning to write *scripts*. And a new form of pornography was unveiled: films that combined full narrative storylines with explicit sex. They were shown not in the shadows, in stag parties or in

△ Georgina Spelvin in *The Devil in Miss Jones* (1972). The film was released in the era of 'porn chic', when pornography emerged from the shadows to discover full narrative storylines and even celebrity.

◁ A collection of 8mm covers from the films of director Lasse Braun, who has been called the 'father of modern pornography' and 'the pope of porn'. He evangelized pornography across Europe in the 1960s in his attempt to get it legalized.

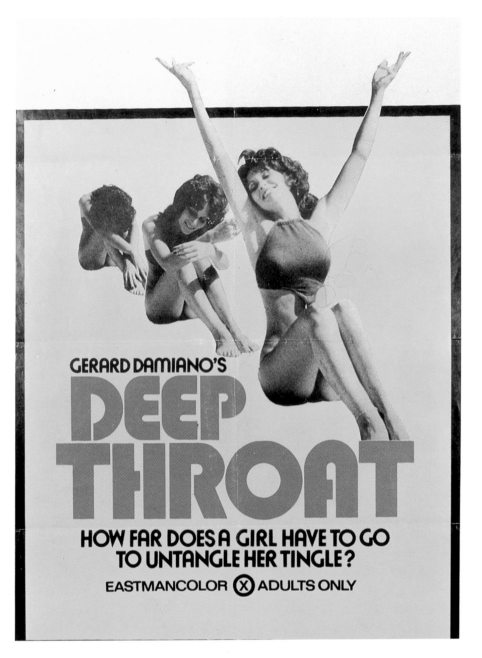

GERARD DAMIANO'S

DEEP THROAT

HOW FAR DOES A GIRL HAVE TO GO TO UNTANGLE HER TINGLE?
EASTMANCOLOR Ⓧ ADULTS ONLY

▷ *Deep Throat* (1972), starring Linda Lovelace, became a box-office phenomenon and the hot subject of late-night television talk shows.

sleazy venues that risked being busted by the police at any moment, but in recognized American theatres. There had never been anything like it, and there would be nothing like it again. Although for a brief moment it looked as if pornography might make it into the mainstream, Porn Chic as it became known – was as short-lived as it was unexpected.

Deep Throat is said to be in the top ten of the biggest box-office successes of all time. It cost $25,000 to make and is reputed to have taken over $100 million worldwide. It

◁▽ *Deep Throat*, the story of a woman who finds that her clitoris is in her throat.

opened at the New World Theater in New York in 1972 and, despite early attempts at suppression by the police, it soon became a media event. Once it was a media event, everyone wanted to see it, and once everyone wanted to see it, the police stopped attempting to bust it. It was mentioned on the *Johnny Carson Show*. It was in *Time* magazine. The rich and famous parked their limousines down the block and then queued up with everyone else.

The film had as its premise the fact that the star, played by Linda Lovelace, had her clitoris in her throat and could come only with 'deep throat' fellatio. It was a phallocentric film as well as a perfect male fantasy: she was gagging for it. However, it also raised the question of the problem of female pleasure. What motivates the narrative and the action is one woman's search for pleasure. The stag film or blue movie, where the end-point had been penetration and the climax was the 'meat shot', had been unconcerned with the problematics of female pleasure. The point of the stag was penetration. In its own way, *Deep Throat* brought the issue of female orgasm to the fore.

As Linda Williams says, 'Everybody went to see it. Not because it was a good film. I would argue that it was an important film, although it was a bad film, and it had the most execrable music. Historically it's an important film because all of a sudden the problem of woman's pleasure is there.'

Another huge success was *Behind the Green Door* (1972). Marilyn Chambers, the film's eventual star, recounts how she first got involved in pornography. She had just done some modelling work to advertise Ivory Soap, which was associated with an image of purity.

Then: 'I read an ad in a newspaper one day and it said, now casting for a major motion picture. I thought, well, that's cool. I had no idea what I was getting myself into. I went down to this place in San Francisco. And I walked in with my little modelling book, and the forms said do you want a balling or a non-balling role. And I didn't know what it meant. I said, "Well, I can bowl." They went, "No, you going to ball or not?"' After an initial hesitation, she signed up. 'I was scared. The sex really didn't worry me as much as what my parents were going to think. I didn't want to embarrass my very British middle-class parents. I didn't want to embarrass anybody. The first day on set everyone's smoking pot. And I didn't even want to know the script. In the story I was playing a woman who is kidnapped and taken to this bizarre sex club and loved as she's never been loved before. So that's how I wanted to play it, as that woman. I

△◁ *Behind the Green Door* (1972), starring Marilyn Chambers. Chambers, who had modelled for Ivory Soap, was another unlikely new star of hard-core.

▷ *Behind the Green Door* (1972) tells the story of a woman who is kidnapped and taken to a sex club: while its star still says today that 'it was really cool', even in these days of revisionism the storyline remains problematic for feminists.

was in a movie, but I was living my life in this movie. And it worked for me. It was really cool. And these women come out from behind the door, the green door, and they start licking my pussy. And then Johnny Keyes, the black guy, came out, and I knew my father was definitely going to kill me. There came a point when it turned from fear to lust. It really turned me on. It was that moment in my life where my life changed. Right then, you saw it. You got to see it.'[21]

SF DISTRIBUTORS *present*
SYLVIA KRISTEL *as* **Emmanuelle** Colour X

The age of Porn Chic made celebrities of the performers. Chambers again: 'When I did *Behind the Green Door* I was a movie star and I rode around in limousines and drank the best champagne and stayed at the Plaza and people stood in line to see me. It was unbelievable, there were thousands of people standing in line. *Johnny Carson* came to sit in line, because it was so cool, it was chic. It was our society telling us that the sexual revolution had reached its peak. It was something that was really, really exciting and we were all part of it and this was a cool thing to do and watch.' Almost overnight, the hounded world of porn had become celebrated.

The Devil in Miss Jones (1972) tells the story of a woman who commits suicide – a big mistake in an otherwise sinless if dull life, as she finds when she is barred from Heaven and destined for Hell. Having sinned so little in her life, and finding she is still bound for Hell anyway, she asks to have her life over again to make it really sinful. She sets about things with huge and lusty enthusiasm. But there is a catch. In the process of developing a huge appetite for all things sexual, her hunger outstrips her ability to be satisfied and this drives her mad. She has acquired an itch that cannot be scratched and she has earned her hell. As Georgina Spelvin recalls: 'I was touring, making personal

△ *Emmanuelle* (1974), starring Sylvia Kristel. Sexual revolution and porn chic had pushed the boundaries sufficiently to allow the general release into the mainstream of sexually adventurous films like *Emmanuelle*. Several years later, in a different climate, the censors recalled the film to cut out a rape scene.

△ *Last Tango in Paris* (1972), starring Marlon Brando and Maria Schneider. One paper at the time said that this film would 'knock the bottom out of the back-street porno market'.

appearances with the film as a semi-vaudeville gig, after it had opened and made something of a splash. One town where I attended the opening and was waiting in the lobby to talk with people and sign autographs and that sort of thing, a pair of nuns came out of the audience and I didn't know whether to run and hide. I'm standing there – I travelled with this pet snake and the snake is around my neck – and these nuns came over to talk with me, and they were so charming, and they said that they had come to see the film because they had heard that it was, indeed, a moral play, and that they found it to be so, and they congratulated me on my acting.'

In such surreal moments, it seemed that pornography was losing its dirty-raincoats image, and was ready to break out of the secret museum. Ultimately, however, the sexual utopia of pornography anarchists like Lasse Braun would remain the 'no-place' of all utopias. And those who had been dreaming of a world reconfigured on different sexual lines, or even new, exciting careers, would get a rude awakening. 'It came crashing to a halt very soon,' says Marilyn Chambers, 'and then it became not cool. It became very uncool to watch porno films. It became dirty. I felt taking a chance doing that would lead to other things – bigger and better things. Boy, was I wrong.' Porn remained firmly in the ghetto and ultimately, despite the heady possibilities presaged by talk of the sexual revolution, it did not lose its stigma. Even those who were in the vanguard of bringing pornography into public view on the 'nothing wrong with sex' platform recognize this. As Alex deRenzy says, 'My daughter used to say, "Dad, if you're the porno King, does that make my sister and I the porno princesses?" I said, "Jeez, I hope not."'

The 1970s would later be seen by those in the American pornography industry as a golden age. Heady 1960s talk of sexual freedom was translated into a wholesale commodification of sex in a new and massive industry. There was a decade of theatrical releases of pornographic feature films on 35mm. In 1980, 6 per cent of the total number of cinemas – about 800 – attracting 3 million paying customers, specialized in showing hard-core porn. Production costs were between $100,000 and $250,000 and producers could count on grossing $1 million in the first eighteen months after release, with an inbuilt longevity that outstripped the normal Hollywood fare.[22] Pornography was big business.

However, it was soon back in its box – a video box, as it turned out, for the future of porn was video. The new medium provided for privacy, choice and control. But the economics of video were quite different. Budgets plummeted, artistic pretensions floundered and dreams of joining the mainstream evaporated for good.

△ *Last Tango in Paris* (1972). One of the most notorious sex scenes in mainstream cinematic history – the butter and buggery scene.

Sex Lives on Videotape

[*Chapter Six: Video**]
by Fenton Bailey

The story goes that Sony's technically superior Betamax format lost out to the rival VHS because they refused to allow it to be used for adult videos. Sony launched their player in 1975 and for a year they had the market to themselves, selling 30,000 units. Then came JVC's VHS and supposedly hordes of porn-starved consumers rushed out and bought players and cassettes. There were other formats competing in this battle too. Zenith had Video 2000 and Philips pushed a tape that could be flipped over, like their audio cassette. Perhaps the biggest loser was RCA with their Selectavision format. In 1969, way ahead of the competition, they excitedly announced a revolutionary new system that would 'play programmes pre-recorded on tapes of clear plastic similar to that used in supermarkets to wrap and display meats'.[1] The press release contained a sample of tape that looked like something out of *Brainstorm:* 'The faint iridescent patterns on the surface of the tape are Fraunfhofer holograms; the images encoded in the holograms are reconstructed when illuminated by coherent light from a laser. [It is] virtually indestructible under conditions of normal use.' But despite investing hundreds of millions of dollars, Selectavision barely made it to market, and together with the other formats would become also-rans in the great stand-off between Betamax and VHS. For a while it looked like the two formats would coexist, but in early 1988 Sony finally conceded defeat when it announced that it would launch its own line of VHS machines.

Although it's a good story, there is no evidence that Sony prevented the format being used for adult material. Instead Betamax lost out to sheer marketing bad luck and perhaps also to some degree a competitive price war. But the grain of truth around

◁ *The Crew Watches Anna Work,* Ken Probst, 1995.

---

* All quotes in this chapter are taken from interviews for the Channel 4 series unless otherwise indicated.

which the myth is spun is that porn was a factor in the speed with which video swept into the home. In 1979 less than 1 per cent of American homes had a video cassette recorder; within ten years more than half of all US homes would.[2] At least initially, the majority of titles available on video were adult. From a porn consumer's perspective, video had instant appeal. Before home video, people had to go out in public to an adult theatre. The risk of exposure, the risk of unwelcome attention and, if caught masturbating in public, the risk of arrest were all very real. True, the avid consumer could always purchase an 8mm film projector and screen loops at home, but not only were these expensive, they also had no sound and the projectors, in addition to being clumsy things to operate and apt to jam, were hardly discreet.

The advent of video took many by surprise and rewarded the early adopters. In 1981 Edward de Roo was a film developer working in the adult business. Up front he ran a restaurant deli, while out back he kept his film baths. One night over dinner with his girlfriend Linda, who was sales manager in an electronics company, he told her about a new medium. She had no idea what video was but, fed up with her current job, decided to take a chance and join Eddy in the new venture.

For Eddy this was a traumatic time: 'My whole life was crumbling away in front of me and this new evil videotape was taking its place. Since 1969 I'd been working with film. I'd been building up equipment, buying a machine here, buying a machine there – it was my life. And here it was disappearing at a rapid pace. And I didn't know if video was just going to be a flash in the pan or not.'

The first challenge was to transfer their film loops to video. At the time film-to-tape telecine was barely existent and prohibitively expensive, so they

△ RCA thought they had the future all sewn up with their Selectavision video disk and videotape system. How wrong they were.

simply projected their films on to the side of their fridge and recorded them on to video. There was no sound, so they built a makeshift booth and overdubbed the oohs and ahhs themselves. The quality was appalling. When they weren't panting out their home-made soundtracks, Eddy worked all night duping with his twelve Betamax decks while Linda would sell all day, cold-calling motels that screened hard-core.

For them the changeover from film to video was instant. As Linda recalls, 'I literally sold 8mm one day and got on the phone to the same customer the next day and sold him video. It was an overnight transition.'

To her and Eddy's surprise, the material sold like hot cakes. 'If I was scared before video, then I was just as scared afterwards. The amounts of money coming into the company were incredible.' Despite the rewards, though, Eddy remains a film romantic. 'Since then videotape has been a vehicle for making money, but it's never replaced my love for film. When you hold it, film has a worth, a soul, a certain magnetism. Video is

just this plastic shell; it's a cheap piece of crap.' On his passport, Eddy still lists himself as a film technician.

Resented as a cheap money-spinning version of film, the advent of video was extremely unwelcome to auteur-directors, who saw themselves as an élite belonging to a grand cinematic tradition. Film director Ron Sullivan, who, in a career spanning thirty years, has directed over 500 features by his count, recalls, 'We liked what we had. We were a very élite crowd. We were movie-makers as pornographers, and there was only a handful of us'. Bill Higgins, another film director who founded the gay video company Catalina, fondly remembers the glory days of film when, with only a limited number of features released every year, opening nights were Hollywood-style affairs with red carpets and beautiful stars. He blames the theatres themselves for starting the rot when they bought video projection systems to get around the expense of having to rent film prints from the distributors. It was, he argues, only a matter of time before customers realized that they too could purchase or rent videotapes and watch them at home instead of having to go out to the theatres.

The next step in video's rapid evolution was to shoot direct to video. Initially this was inconvenient and not nearly as good as film. As Bill Higgins recalls, 'Early video had

△ A promotional picture from 1972 for an RCA black-and-white video camera: 'instant taping of home-movie scenes will be possible . . . And if the cameraman flubs the scene, just re-shoot over the tape'.

JANUARY 1981 $1.50

HOME VIDEO

MARILYN CHAMBERS
Video Sex Goddess

SEX AND VIDEO:
A SPECIAL REPORT

Molly Haskell on the Past and Present

Isaac Asimov on the Future

X-Rated Acts:
► **Videotaping in the Boudoir**
► **How the Mob Controls Video Pornography and Piracy**
► **How Sex Plays on Cable TV**

Test Report: Magnavox Camera

△ Marilyn Chambers easily managed the transition from porn film star to 'video sex goddess'.

▷ Director Ron Sullivan on set. With over 500 films to his credit, he has become used to shooting and directing his films in one day.

a very harsh look to it. There was a little line that would go around people's ears and their heads. These cameras also had a tendency to look through layers of flesh, so you could see all of the blemishes underneath. We had to use very heavy make-up.'

Problems of quality aside, these would prove to be halcyon days for the early pioneers in the medium, at least financially. There was a huge demand with only limited supply. Bill Higgins, with just $750 to his name, spent most of it on a mail-order advertisement for his film *Boys of Venice* in the gay weekly *The Advocate*. When he went to check his post office box he found orders totalling $80,000. He had never had it so good – and, he adds wryly, would never have it so good again.

Fast-forward twenty years and video has swept all before it. Although today some titles are still shot on film, they are the notable exceptions rather than the rule. The bulky and hard-to-use formats like Low Band U-Matic have given way to small, easy-to-use camcorders that fit in the palm of your hand, which is all that a director often needs. Thanks to digital technology, these small-format tapes are broadcast quality.

Bill Higgins lives in semi-retirement in Prague, directing high-gloss features shot on small-format digital video. He spends months working over these labours of love. 'The cameras have really advanced. They're very easy to operate, they're easy to hold, and you have a lot of control that you didn't have with the video cameras we started out with ten years ago. They've also added what I would call a beauty chip to these little cameras that just make skin look absolutely fantastic.'

Meanwhile, back in California, Ron Sullivan is shooting *True Prostitute Stories*. He was encouraged to return to directing by his two sons, both of whom are adult video directors, and by the advent of digital video. Films that previously took weeks to shoot can now be shot in a day: 'One day I got up in the morning thinking, I'm shooting a video today and I've just got one day to do it. Somewhere across town, some kid about half my age is springing out of bed thinking, I'm making a movie today and I've got all day to do it.'

Ron relishes being back in control. He is both director and cameraman, and his wife assists, nonchalantly moving in with a fluorescent light also known as the cosy spot to illuminate those hard to reach but crucial nooks and crannies. Ron readily admits that it was the romance and status of film that prejudiced him and blinded him to video's very real advantages. 'There is an immediacy about video that you can't get with film. You lose the show-business quality of film; there's no big crew or massive set-ups, no caterers, no trucks, no trailers, and with fewer people involved, the hotter and the more genuine the sex – it's more intimate. The truth is that video is better for pornography than film ever was. No one likes to admit it because we felt we were giving up too much of our craft. But we've just gone to a better, faster medium, and now it's easy for anybody to do it.'

The result is no less than the creation of another Hollywood behind the Hollywood sign. The twenty-mile strip of the San Fernando Valley has come to be known as Porno Valley and, less charitably, Silicone Valley. It is here, nestling in the bedroom communities of Canoga, Chatsworth and Van Nuys, that the majority of America's hard-core porn is produced. Over 100 companies, like Vivid, Metro, VCA, Evil Empire, Elegant Angel, Wicked and Cabbalero, cluster around the western outreaches of the Los Angeles conurbation, where business-park warehouses give way to the huge boulders and scrub of desert.

Only in the last twenty years has this other Hollywood become the centre of the adult porn business. Historically, San Francisco and New York were the twin poles. But in 1985 West Coast porn director Hal Freeman decided to fight back against a police raid that had resulted in his arrest and shut down one of his productions. In those days the police raided sets routinely. But in this instance they charged the actors with prostitution and Freeman with pandering. Freeman decided against pleading guilty and fought the case, arguing that since pornography was not illegal in the States, it must therefore be legal to produce it, even if that meant paying people to have sex. The California Supreme Court decided that making a movie that involved sexual situations and paying the actors was a legitimate endeavour and was not prostitution. After this victory LA, with its warmer winters than New York and sunnier climate than San Francisco, became the natural home for making adult videos year round.

Zane Entertainment is a typical example of one of the many Mom and Pop family-run operations thriving in

Porno Valley. Chuck Zane started out in the business in 1971, aged twenty-one, building up a chain of half a dozen retail stores. In 1986, because of a clampdown on the retail market, he moved into production. Based in Rochester in up-state New York, he soon realized that trying to run his business from the East Coast made no sense, so he relocated in 1991 to the north-west corner of the valley. Today he has 15,000 square feet of offices and warehousing, and enjoys a turnover of about $5 million, releasing about fifty new titles a year and between thirty and forty compilation tapes on top of that. Three of his kids work for him: Denise (twenty-one) is his assistant, while Matt (twenty-four) and Marc (twenty-two) direct: 'They make 'em, I sell 'em,' he explains.

Porno Valley even has dedicated soundstages specializing in the production of adult movies. Such operations are well suited to the conveyor-belt mentality of the place, where the average movie is shot in a day and a half on a budget of $20,000. Jay Shanahan runs the Stage, which, for $1,500 a day, offers clients five standard sets and a bar set-up. Bedrooms and bars are the most popular 'because everything can start and end in a bar.' For extra money the stage also offers specialized sets such as hospital wards and jail cells: 'We can do pretty much anything and tailor it to your budget.' Recently strip clubs have been popular. In the course of a year they expect to handle about 150 productions, or around three a week.

Since 1991 Porno Valley has also been home to *Adult Video News*, the industry's trade magazine, which started out in Philadelphia in 1983 as a sixteen-page giveaway. Since then the magazine has grown with the adult video market, and now averages 300 pages an issue. It aims to review every new title released. In 1998 this peaked at a staggering 8,948 titles, in a business grossing – including sales and rentals – $4.1 billion.

Meanwhile, in Europe there is no Porno Valley. Instead, with the sole exception of Great Britain, the porn business is an interconnected network spread across the Continent. The Swedish company Private (which recently set a precedent as the first

◁▽ The Hot d'Or Awards. (Left) Tabitha Cash, porn film star, arrives with her incredible bodyguards. (Below) The awards ceremony.

adult company to go public with a stock offering) is headquartered in Barcelona. Scala, Europe's largest distributor, with an annual turnover of $50 million, shipping to thirty-two countries, has its massive warehouse and wholesale showroom on an industrial estate in Amsterdam. Every month managing director Jan Schijff drives his top-of-the-range Mercedes two and half hours to Silwa, in Germany's Ruhr Valley, a state-of-the-art facility where much of their dubbing is done. With 4,000 video recorders, Silwa can duplicate 50,000 tapes a day from any one of the 40,000 masters in their vault: operations are monitored from a control room that would not look out of place in Houston's mission control. And because no feature film is ever a standard length, Silwa has its own cassette production line, where tape the precise length of a movie is spooled into cassette shells.

As in America, when video first appeared in Europe hardcore was illegal, with the exception of Denmark. Film and video producers and distributors were outlaws running underground operations. Jan Schijff served eighteen months in a British prison after he was caught smuggling in a consignment of porn. Gradually, as the law changed and as video became more commonplace, these pirate operations have graduated into high-tech businesses, using state-of-the-art equipment, computer inventorying, just-in-time delivery and the kind of management systems you would expect to find in a car factory.

On both sides of the Atlantic there is no greater evidence of this dramatic change than the black tie occasions when the American and European industries hold their

△ Models from Private at a photocall during the Cannes Film festival.

▷ The Hot d'Or Awards. (Top sequence) A winner walks up to collect her award. (Bottom) The 1992 ceremony.

respective versions of the Academy Awards. In January the Adult Video News Awards are held in Las Vegas, while the Hot d'Or holds its awards in Cannes during the film festival. Both ceremonies are very similar, even down to the identical design of the coveted gilded trophies, and both resemble the Oscars, as female stars in glittering jewels and evening gowns make their way through a flurry of camera flashes to a podium where they make teary-eyed acceptance speeches.

*

Those who thought video would be a flash in the pan and dismissed it as some cheap version of film dramatically underestimated how profoundly different video was as a medium. It might have been cheap but in its very cheapness lay several crucial differences that would make video responsible for the creation in less than twenty-five years of a multi-billion-dollar international industry.

The scale of video was completely different from film. Camille Paglia attended the première of *Deep Throat* and found the gargantuan projection of genitalia more akin to plumbing than the erotic. As Professor Henry Jenkins, director of media studies at the Massachusetts Institute of Technology, notes, 'A ten-foot tall cum shot is something to see. It looks like an enormous fountain erupting in our midst, but it isn't real. Whereas porn on video brings things down to a human scale.' The gritty warts-and-all reality contrasted with the transcendent nature of the cinematic experience: 'Because film is so vivid at conveying properties of light, the bodies on film were extraordinarily beautiful, but they're removed from the world that the rest of us live in. They're glowing visions up on the screen, and they can be extraordinarily spectacular. Cinema focuses on the gleam, on the surface of sex.'

Film, projected on to a giant screen, aspired to the ideal. And so perhaps it was no surprise that the adult film world mimicked Hollywood high-profile premières. 'Theatrical hard-core shot on film is a genre that's trying for legitimacy. It wants to be like a commercial Hollywood narrative film. It wants to be like a film, so you have your writing, your action, your climax, your resolution. Once you get to video, however, things change, because it's a different medium,' says Jay Lorenz, a teacher at Irving University, California.

Video, transmitted on a television screen a fraction of the size, aspired to nothing. Instead it was a scaled-down reflection of reality.

Perhaps the easiest way to understand the differences between the two media is to look at how they were produced. Video gave directors the option of changing the grammar of film-making, a language largely dictated by film's technical requirements and overall expense. Before filming a scene, it was necessary to block it out; to determine where the performer would be in relation to the camera. Having covered the action with a wide or master shot, it was then necessary to reposition the camera and reset the lights to get close-ups of the same action, each shot requiring a new set-up. Camcorders dispensed with this need. With auto-exposure, auto-focus and auto-steady functions, all the

director had to do was point and shoot. And whereas film was expensive, videotape was cheap, so the director, instead of continually having to stop and stage the action, could just let it roll and allow the sex to take its natural course, document-ing the action as it unfolded in one continuous take. In sum, where film lent itself to elaborate script-led narrative features, video suggested a more documentary, non-linear approach. Who even needed a script?

And film, because of the overall expense of producing a feature,

△ *Breast Fondling*, Ken Probst, 1995.

needed to recoup that investment by appealing to the widest possible audience. 'You had heterogeneous entertainment for heterogeneous audiences. You had to show something that appealed to everyone, and, therefore, minority tastes are pushed to the side,' explains Henry Jenkins. While film was obliged to aspire to the ideal, video, because it was infinitely less expensive, could afford to go niche and downmarket, documenting sex that would appeal to some and not to others. What the medium lacked in its ambition to portray idealized sexual perfection, it would more than make up for with its insatiable appetite for documenting the full range of sexual function, or dysfunction, as the medium also provided an opportunity for extremism.

As Jay Lorenz says, 'The video gaze is different from the film gaze. There's always other things happening around you when you are watching television, but when you go to see a movie everything around you is black. You're looking at a huge screen, your focus is there. When you're watching TV, it can never really be a gaze. It's more of a glance. However, sometimes the glance becomes a hard gaze – pun intended.'

As worthy of no more than a mere glance, video might have been a lame-duck medium were it not for the magician's wand of remote control. After his attempted assassination attempt on Ronald Reagan, gunman John Hinckley commented, 'This gun gives me pornographic power', presumably meaning that it intoxicated him with a sexual power. The quasi-phallus of the remote control is a similar kind of joystick, empowering and even arousing the bearer. Camille Paglia sees that, 'the remote control with its fetishistic and phallic quality has a kind of organic element to it that was not present in the purely visual activity of watching television with the family. The VCR becomes a kind of companion. My theory is that it's part of the hunting instinct that descends from primitive times. The man in finding the juicy part of a porn video is really hunting out a deer or a rabbit. There is a carnivorous aspect to it.' The remote fundamentally alters our relationship to television, giving us the power to direct the way we view something and making the experience a genuinely interactive one. No longer slave to real time or narrative, we can fast-forward, hunting down particular moments. By replaying those moments over and over, or by searching through them frame by frame, the viewer is able to prolong pleasure by repeating certain moments and subjecting them not to a glance but to a hard gaze of intense scrutiny. In this way the visible is rendered even more visible.

Armed with the magic wand, if it was no longer necessary to sit through a story, why bother with the story at all? After a brief attempt to mimic the film world with its features and stars, video began developing its own post-narrative formats that internalized the work of the remote control. Particularly popular are compilation tapes consisting of sexual highlights and orgasmic moments lifted out of regular features and strung together to create a 'greatest hits package'. Compilations are enormously popular, constituting two-thirds of all releases in 1998.

What Jay Lorenz called 'sexual numbers with a minor framing story' is the key to another video-only format: the genre known as wall-to-wall, so called because there was nothing else on the tape besides the most minimal of set-ups. Within this genre the subcategory of gang-bang tapes, in which a single girl will have sequential sex with hundreds of men, is particularly popular.

Marathon gang-bang tapes are interesting not only as an illustration of the video dispensing with traditional narrative, but also show the way they strive to turn the TV glance into a hard gaze with attention-grabbing non-stop action. But the approach favoured leads us into uncharted sexual territory. The very notion of a gang-bang goes beyond the limits of what most people might consider normal sexual behaviour. Neither is Annabel Chong, pin-up girl of the genre since setting the record in 1995 by having sex with 251 men, your stereotypical female: 'I don't need to go out on a date and be nice to someone to get laid. I can just fuck, take a shower and go home. People have called me a bimbo and a slut and a whore but I just enjoy my body. I love sex; I need more. Setting the world land sex record seemed like the natural next step.'

Just as Chong bucks gender stereotypes (after all, the popular if ignorant perception is that it is men not women who are sexually insatiable), so *The World's Biggest Gang-Bang* defies heterosexual stereotypes, with its hundreds of penises on parade. While a single money shot can be rationalized as a squirted seal of authenticity in the average adult film, it's hard to apply the same argument to the hundreds of cum shots that run

all the way through the gang-bang. While it has been suggested that the army of penises deconstructs individual members to create a sort of everyman dick out of this cockucopia, there is also something potentially homoerotic about the tape. Indeed, one sees less of the female star than one does of the hundreds of supporting male actors crowding like bees around a solitary honeypot that is more often than not obscured by all the male flesh pressing forward.

*

Video was not only a different medium, it also represented a different kind of sex. It's exploration of non-narrative formats has led it to non-standard sexual representation. Instead of reducing sex to a few tested and tried formulas, video has considerably broadened the repertoire and in so doing crossed sexual boundaries, taboos and stereotypes with gay abandon.

'With film you have such a limited market. You have basically a straight market and a gay market. But with video porn it expands the market where you have bisexual porn, transsexual porn, lesbian porn, foot-fetish porn,' says Jay Lorenz. *AVN* magazine, which reviews tapes by genre, also lists Fat/Pregnant, Tickling, Amateur, Catfights, Old Babes, Spanking and even Anal as separate categories. In particular, the popularity of anal sex is a creation of the video market. As Mark Kernes, features editor of *AVN*, explains, sodomy laws in America meant that depicting anal sex in adult films was always a high risk for the movie houses. But because the same kind of regulatory scrutiny was not applied to the home video market, in the last ten years it has become a staple of home video: 'Now almost every tape has an anal scene and some are just completely devoted to the genre.'

With home video it was no longer necessary to practise sexual apartheid. The anxiety an audience might feel on watching sex that deviated from the norm was not something that producers had to worry about for the one-on-one market. Indeed, safe in the privacy of their own home, viewers might be tempted to explore sexual fantasies and identities by watching tapes they would be too embarrassed to watch when exposed to public view in a theatre. 'Ten or fifteen years ago, the idea of having pornography for straight men that included gay sex would have been absolutely impossible, inconceivable. The cum shot was there, but it was a guilty secret. No one wanted to acknowledge they really looked at someone else's cock when they watched pornography,' says Professor Jenkins. By sparing viewers public shame, video not only sanctioned this but even encouraged experimentation and exploration.

Indeed, the promise of unconventional sex would become a unique selling point for video, especially when in 1991 Eddy and Linda de Roo launched Totally Tasteless Video, an extreme fetish line that began with *Aged to Perfection*, featuring older actors. One tape, *Century Sex*, featuring an eighty-seven-year-old grandmother, was sold with the tag line, 'Boldly go where every man has gone before.' Then they moved on to midgets. 'We only have four midget titles, but I can't keep them on the shelf,' says Linda. 'For some reason gay men love to look at midgets,' adds Eddy.

More To Love, featuring overweight people, most memorably a 600lb woman called Eartha Quake, have also proved popular. But the titles that Eddy is proudest of in the Totally Tasteless line are those featuring pregnant models and lactating women.

▽ Annabel Chong, founder star of the gang-bang marathon genre. 'I don't need to go on dates and be nice to people in order to get laid'.

A long-time fan of avant-garde films, Eddy strives to evoke the same sort of emotional shock from his viewers. 'I'm always looking for different areas to go into, different lines to cross and barriers to break down,' he says apropos another Totally Tasteless speciality, the Buttcam, a twenty-five-inch medical probe with a wide-angle lens and a light. Recently Eddy's magic touch failed him when he seemed to venture too far into the corporeal with *Period Pieces*, which depicted men having sex with menstruating women. Unrepentant, he plans to continue to push the envelope, releasing a tape showing people vomiting.

One particular TTV compilation tape, *Really Gross Anals*, featured a porn star on the cover demonstrating her singular ability to turn her anus inside out. Constance Penley, Professor of Film Studies at the University of California in Santa Barbara, sees this as an example of video porn's Rabelaisian comedy, a celebration of the body that

◁ Chong prepares herself for her record-breaking marathon sex session: 'I love sex; I need more. Setting the world land sex record seemed like the natural next step'.

delights in the grotesque and harks back to the tradition of the circus freak show. 'It's not just the sexualized, eroticized body, it's also the body that farts and pisses and shits. It's a celebration of corporeality in all of its aspects. The attraction for the viewer isn't necessarily an erotic one, but it's one that offers us the chance to be disgusted, to be frightened and to have worries about our own bodies.' Jay Lorenz concurs: 'Pornographic video definitely pursues extreme behaviours. It's related to body songs. It's related to all-men parties where people watch these videos and roar with laughter.' He sees this comic voice as inherent to the medium. 'Pornographic film wanted so much to be a player in terms of mainstream cinema that it took itself almost too seriously. Video can't take itself too seriously, because it doesn't have the budget to take itself too seriously. It therefore tends to be a lot more playful than the films of the 1970s.'

As the name suggests, Totally Tasteless Video is a deliberate and knowing enterprise. Eddy's screen nickname is Loretta, after a character in a Monty Python film. His penchant for the humour of the extreme echoes early John Waters films of the late 1970s. Waters made his name with gross-out films like *Pink Flamingoes* and *Desperate Living*, featuring, among many other things, overweight drag queens eating dog faeces. 'With the X-rated genre you can get absurd. You can get really nasty and icky and just

kind of wallow in muck. And people are going to turn away and go yuk. But that's what I want. That's why I'm making these particular videos. I want them for shock value. I want it to be absurd. I want it to be repulsive,' says Eddy.

But others see in video's extremism and lack of respect for what is normally said, done or shown an ability to generate laughs more knowing than simple gags of disgust. Totally Tasteless, with their obvious delight in extreme scenarios and radical close-ups can be seen as parodying the entire genre of hard-core. The inside-out sphincter and the camera up someone's colon satirize porn's obsession with the visible. By plumbing these depths in this way, the frenzy of the visible becomes the absurdity of the medical.

Elsewhere, video's comic voice critiques everything from Washington to so-called legitimate Hollywood. 'One of my favourite uses of comedy in pornographic films,' says Constance Penley, 'is in the porn knock-offs of Hollywood film and television. As soon as a film comes out you have *Waiting to X-X-X-Hale, The Sperminator,* and *Shaving Ryan's Privates,* a gay male film in which everybody gets shaved by the end of the film. I don't think any of this would have happened without video. Hollywood was never going to risk being more sexually explicit. It can simulate sex, but it can never really give you the sex that the porn videos can.' Penley finds implicit in these films 'a kind of critique of Hollywood film, for its hypocrisies and its pretensions. For the way Hollywood film promises sex, but never delivers, only giving us simulated sex and substituting violence for the sex that it can't deliver.'

She also applauds what she calls tabloid porn, fast turnaround movies ripped from the headlines such as *Sunset and Divine* (the re-enactment of the scandal in which British film star Hugh Grant was caught with a prostitute) and *Uncut* (a porno dramatization of John Wayne Bobbitt's castration by his wife). Most recently released is *Scenes from the Oral Office,* which takes the tabloid tone of the Starr Report one dramatic step further. By the end of the film, characters such as Moanica Lewinsky and Hillary Clit-on enjoy every imaginable sexual combination, including an orgy scene in which Linda Tripp goes down on Janet Reno who is cruelly revealed to be a man in a dress.

As a cheap medium, adult video compensated for this by going where film would not, to extremes, and in so doing found a comic voice that could lampoon the hypocrisies of Washington and the pretensions of Hollywood. Underpinning this licence was the fact that video could document the reality without recourse to artifice, glamour or even nice lighting. Adult video was able to capitalize further on this documentary-style approach after a second wave of video technology breathed new life into an adult industry that was, in the 1980s, in a considerable depression.

In October 1986, just a few months after the Meese Report condemning pornography had been published, an article in *The New York Times* reported that the X-rated industry was in a slump. Only 1,600 adult titles were released that year, down 100 from the previous year. *Playgirl* magazine had filed for bankruptcy and the circulation of *Hustler* magazine was down by a half. Of

Manhattan's sex shops and movie houses, 103 had closed, leaving only forty-four still in business. Half of these were in Times Square and so were threatened by a looming $2 billion redevelopment project.

Were the regulation clamp-downs working? Was the audience losing interest in such tasteless fare? We will never know, because the arrival of the camcorder changed everything. For 1986 was also the year that D1, the first digital video format, came on the market. Affordable to high-end industry users only, in the long-term consumer digital cameras would strengthen the revolution that happened later with the release in 1987 of S-VHS and Hi8. More than simply a boon for a stagnant industry, these new domestic formats would revolutionize the video gaze (or glance) anew, as people began picking up camcorders (as these new all-in-one cameras and recorders came to be known) to record their *own* sex lives on videotape.

These camcorders might have been targeted at the consumer but they could yield professional results, leading some to coin the term 'prosumer'. It is easy to underestimate the emergence of the prosumer camcorder, which effectively reconfigured the pornographic domain. Until this point, there was always a clear distinction between the audience and the producer, between the amateur viewer and the professional performer. Indeed, the entire regulation of pornography is based on a clear distinction between the innocent consumer, who needs to be protected, and the criminal producer. But from now on that distinction would begin to lose its clarity. 'I think the camcorder changed the television monitor from a receive-only passive medium into a medium for self-expression. We now see the television monitor as a portal, as a place to express who we are. So, in a lot of television, whether it be *Cops* or *Jerry Springer,* we want to see things that reflect the raw reality of our lives rather than these airbrushed *Playboy*-style images of an über-culture of stars,' says New York University professor Doug Rushkoff, who has written several books detailing our relationship with the media.

One of many people who have crossed the line from consumer to producer is Farrell Timlake, a Washington graduate with an interest in performance art. 'My wife and I used to watch porn videos, but we were charmed by these things called Homegrown Videos. They were very different from the adult videos because these tapes weren't in colourful boxes, just simple black and white sleeves and consisted of people making their own home movies and sending them in. It shocked us because these were real people just having sex, and without all the corny dialogue and stuff that we hated.'

Farrell and his wife decided that they would make their own tape. One night after a Grateful Dead concert they made their first tape in the bathroom of their Las Vegas hotel. It amused them so much that they realized they were 'born to porn' and showed it the next day to their friends. Then they sent it to Homegrown. But Homegrown didn't buy the tape because the company was bankrupt. When Timlake and his wife found out, they scraped enough money together to buy it and today Homegrown is one of the largest amateur video

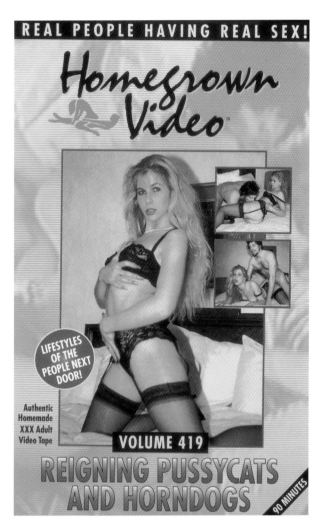

REAL PEOPLE HAVING REAL SEX!

Homegrown Video™

LIFESTYLES OF THE PEOPLE NEXT DOOR!

Authentic Homemade XXX Adult Video Tape

VOLUME 419

REIGNING PUSSYCATS AND HORNDOGS

90 MINUTES

△ Homegrown Videos: America's most revealing home videos.

companies. They have a library of some 500 tapes and pay $20 a minute to punters who send in their home videos for distribution. Normally about five or six vignettes make up a Homegrown title.

Quite deliberately Homegrown is not based in Porno Valley, and Farell feels some antipathy to the other Hollywood, where he did a brief stint as a wannabe porn star before finding his calling in amateur. 'On a typical San Fernando set it's "OK, you're gonna be in these positions, then we're gonna cut to the anal scene and then the pop shot on your face", and it's that same thing over and over. I call it the McDonald Syndrome, because they're making the same cheeseburger. But in an amateur film you see the evolution of the sexual dynamic, you see when people start to get turned on, you see the flush on the face and the sweat on the cheek and you know something has really happened. In a typical San Fernando they cut right after they come. But in amateur tapes people want to see the afterglow. People generally want to think of sex as having humour and passion and amateur videos really show that. People can relate to that experience much more than they can relate to these big "Fuck me, fuck me, baby" scripted scenes that don't really make sense to a lot of people.'

Amateur has not so much rewritten the rules and formulas as simply thrown them out. It has overturned the supremacy of the cum or money shot. As Linda Williams has written in *Hard Core: Power, Pleasure and the 'Frenzy of the Visible'*[3], the male ejaculation while serving as ocular proof that pleasure has taken place, is also a kind of artifice. This special performance for the benefit of the camera confirms that these are not real people consorting for their own pleasure but actors hired to perform for ours.

Farrell, who often lets himself be guided by the letters he gets from his consumers, says people do not want external money shots: 'They say I want to see sex like I really have it at home. They may have tried to come on a woman's face and they got what a real woman would say to him and it's not pleasant.'

I really enjoyed your *Cream Pie for Dessert*. Please do another. I am tired of endless blow-jobs and spraying cum.

I like brunettes, droopy tits and unshaven pussies. Coming inside a female turns me on. Then seeing it drip out. That's why *Cream Pie* is my favorite video. I would appreciate you producing more *Cream Pie* videos.

Similarly, amateurs are not interested in the standard issue body beautiful that California has perfected. As Farrell has found, 'What the amateur video teaches us is that what people want is something real. And an older woman on the plump side with a hairy pussy and large, drooping breasts, that's real. And people like that. One of our most popular titles is *Oversexed, Overweight and Over Forty*. That's the goddess. That's the woman everyone wants.'

I live in a farm region and most of the farmers dig chubby, oversexed, mature women dressed seductively. That is, wearing nylons and high-heel shoes actively engaged in fucking, sucking and taking it up the ass.

The same lack of emphasis on the perfection of the body is mirrored in the lack of high production values. The critical factor is not what is seen, but how real it is. Indeed, the lack of production values signifies the real. As Professor Jenkins explains, 'All pornography is a documentary in that what you're watching is something that really happened. And the bad production values, the lousy lighting, the wavering sound quality, and the way the actors suddenly jump up and adjust the camera mid-process, all those communicate the fact that this was real sex between real people who normally don't get paid for it and who are sharing their most intimate experiences with us for our viewing pleasure. Once you get actors with implants having sex on perfectly lit stages in glamorous environments, then it ceases to have reality.'

The very first amateur in the business was Ugly George. Ugly George is something of a legend on the streets of New York, where he used to prowl with his video camera in the 1970s, looking for women he could lure into a dark alley and talk into flashing him (and his inseparable video camera) their breasts. And sometimes more.

He started out as a hapless freelance photographer with a knack for finding talent but not for taking pictures. The editors of the nudie magazines he worked for told him, 'You have absolutely no talent as a photographer. But the way you pick up these girls is fantastic. We've never seen girls like this. How do you do it?' So he told them: 'I would be walking down the street, see a beautiful girl, go over and start uh, chatting her up. And start talking to her. And many times it would happen that she'd go with me someplace. We'd get off the street, get her panties down and I'd start to take some pictures.' Contrary to all expectation, an amazing number of people would indulge his requests.

In the early 1970s George made the transition from photography to video, buying a bulky black and white Sony Portapak, which he mounted on his back. This, combined with a silver jumpsuit, made him a wacky Manhattan fixture. In fact, according to George, Bill Murray once told him he was the inspiration for the Ghostbuster outfits in the blockbuster movie.

George claims that his public access cable show, which aired three times a week, scooped a 66 per cent share of all cable homes in the New York area: 'Technically

△ One man and his
camera: video pioneer,
Ugly George.

speaking, and financially speaking, it was the worst show on television. It was the only black and white show on television. Poor editing. Poor sound. Poor camera work. But the people loved the way I picked up the women. They loved that. They were saying, if this ugly Polish peasant with no money can pick up women and get them to pose nude, there's hope for me. I can do it too.'

Ugly George's significance is that his work bestrides two distinct genres of video, anticipating both by almost fifteen years. On the one hand, he was the first amateur. Instead of making millions out of his innovative show, George remained a committed amateur. Today he still lives in what he calls a Polish penthouse, a single tiny room above a nightclub, heating tins of food on one ring, sleeping on a couch surrounded by his array of video equipment. At the same time, he is also the grandfather of pro-am, a genre that more than any other drives today's adult video market.

Pro-am was the video industry's response to the perceived threat of amateur. Pro-am is distinct from amateur in that it normally features a professional interacting with an amateur. Often the professional is cameraman and director and the so-called amateur is also a professional such as a stripper or escort. This genre is also known as Gonzo, a term first borrowed by Mark Kernes of *AVN* magazine from the shaggy-dog-style journalism of Hunter S. Thompson's *Fear and Loathing in Las Vegas*, and John Stagliano is widely acknowledged as its inventor.

In the early 1980s Stagliano was a male stripper who felt he was going nowhere. As he tells it, the thing that transformed his fortunes was buying one of the new camcorders. Suddenly he was a director. Of course, in the days before video it would have taken him years to break into the rarefied and exclusive world of film directors – if he had been able to do so at all. By his own admission, his first effort was not very good, but because there was such demand and so little video product on the market at the time, it sold well enough to get him into the business. Today he heads Evil Angel, a company that represents and distributes a number of other key producers of Gonzo.

Like so many others who work in the adult video business, John Stagliano is not some stereotypical sleazy wheeler dealer. He is quiet, polite and particularly modest. On screen he has a humorous persona that has led Constance Penley to call him the Woody Allen of porn: 'His character is this hapless guy who is helplessly in thrall to his passion for finding the world's most perfect butt. He often fails in his efforts and that becomes part of the story. It's not just the quest of some perfect man to find some perfect sexual situation. It's the quest of a fairly ordinary guy to try and find sexual satisfaction and recognition.'

Stagliano realized that with this camera he had total freedom not only to shoot whatever he wanted but also to escape the stale mould of porn features: 'In the 1980s, we were writing these stupid scripts on these low budgets and actors were required to utter lines when they couldn't even act. The great thing about Gonzo is that I can direct from behind the camera and I can deal in a more naturalistic style so that people, when they're looking right at the camera, are just talking to me and being themselves.'

Academics like Jay Lorenz see Gonzo as a stake through the heart of narrative. 'We're seeing a return to spectacle. We're seeing mainstream films come out like *Speed* that have no plot and no characterization and rely on a series of set pieces. John Stagliano's Gonzo films are doing

the same thing, giving you the same set-up over and over and over and over again with the emphasis on the spectacle.' As Mark Kernes elaborates, 'Basically it's a stream of consciousness, a kind of journalism that can go any place and doesn't follow the linear path that a regular story would follow.'

△ *Buttman in Rio*: an example of John Stagliano's 'Gonzo' genre of home-movie-style videos.

Instead Gonzo often takes the form of a travelogue, and in this respect continues to develop video's documentary drive and tendency to include all shapes and sizes as part of mapping the real. 'We watch his compatriots have sex with foreign women that they've found in this exotic land,' says Jay Lorenz 'so it tends to be a travelogue not necessarily of places but of female bodies. Gonzo in this sense is showcasing new female flesh. Eastern Europe is a place where, for Americans anyway, women were not sexualized. They were thought of in disparaging terms as being unattractive. Now that Communism has fallen, what do we do? We go in and we sexualize them. We say, no, no, no, these women are attractive. They can be corporal commodities as well.'

But video is not just interested in sexually commodifying those formerly behind the Iron Curtain for cynical exploitation by the man next door. Increasingly the man next door is using video to sexually commodify himself as well.

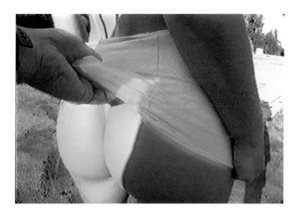

△ Gonzo has become the most popular genre of adult video, accounting for an estimated sixty per cent of the market.

It is ironic that video as a medium should be doing this. After all, when it was initially introduced it was a way of taking the pornographic experience as something public and privatizing it. But now people are taking this private medium that can be used to record their most private moments and publicizing them. Doug Rushkoff feels our traditional notions of privacy need re-evaluation in the light of this exhibitionism: 'I think people are becoming more and more aware of the fact that we live in a surveillance culture. And it changes the way people regard their privacy and their sense of identity. If you live in a world where you know almost everything you're doing is being recorded, then in an odd way the way for you to experience your personal space is by doing exhibitionist things, because then you can experience the barrier between public and private.' In other words, privacy, traditionally seen as something to be preserved at all costs, is now something to be tested and tasted. Take the example of Pamela Lee Anderson, the *Baywatch* star, who has on occasion been camera-shy and maintained her right to privacy. At the same time, her home-made sex video with partner, Tommy Lee, is widely available. Of course, it only seems a paradox; even non-celebrities who explicitly expose and exploit their sex lives still expect to have the right to a private life.

The notion of making one's own sex video – whether for private or public use – has become such a commonplace that an Australian television show recently included a feature guiding viewers on how to make better home-sex videos, including tips on setting the mood with lighting and music, choosing a location, using a tripod and a final reminder to take the tape out of the camera after use.

Freelance journalist Dean Kuipers, who was commissioned by *Playboy* to write a feature on the amateur video revolution, decided that the only way to do this was to make his own amateur video. He found that in the process the sex was dramatically altered, becoming somehow charged: 'It's not just a recording device. It's a symbol of someone's presence in a greater world, an electronic world,' he said. Having made the videotape, when he played it back he discovered a new persona on the screen. 'We have all made sex symbols out of the stars that we see on television and at the movies and part of their power is simply that they're on the screen. So if you can tape yourself, then you become one of those people who has somehow gathered all that magnetic, erotic

power that comes from just having their image replicated through electronic means. You've replicated your image electronically. And that's powerful stuff.'

Similarly, others found that the presence of the camera in the room changed the dynamic. 'The camera was an extra voyeuristic partner, and when you realize that this mechanical partner can tell that story to your friends and entertain others, well, that definitely adds a drama to the whole moment,' says Farrell Timlake, recalling his first home-made film. Doug Rushkoff also adds, 'It elevates the sex act from the ephemeral world and pedestrian realm to one worthy of being recorded.'

People are not just making love to one another in front of a camera, they are making love to the camera, and the results of this kind of intercourse have altered both the nature of the camera and the people using the cameras. In much the same way as the remote control, the video camera 'has become a sexualized instrument. It contains magical properties or fetishistic properties because of your link to it in terms of desire,' says Jay Lorenz. In short, our relationship with video is far more complex than it is with other media technologies. For the video camera, in addition to being a tool enabling us to express ourselves, is also a hybrid of sex toy and sex partner.

In his 1983 film *Videodrome*, David Cronenberg explores this notion of video co-dependence. 'The television screen has become the retina of the mind's eye,' says Dr Brian O'Blivion, the film's mad scientist. This evolutionary kink manifests itself when James Woods develops a vaginal slit in his stomach into which he inserts videotapes. Cronenberg's conceit is that the electronic reality of television and video is more real than the lesser reality of real life.

While people may not be acquiring anything as extreme as video-slit stigmata, amateurs, increasingly well versed in the traditions of professional porn, are behaving more and more like porn stars. At Homegrown, Farrell has noticed that people are more self-conscious in the tapes they send in about themselves: 'People really do try to be more like porn stars. It's more extreme sex now. It just used to be kind of standard missionary, and now it's every kind of fetish and kink that you can imagine. They cut the foreplay and move into the real action.'

Cronenberg's vision is, of course, the stuff of horror films rather than reality, and Matt Zane, the self-proclaimed director of Generation-X porn, has not even seen

Videodrome. However, he unconsciously echoes Cronenberg's vision of the new cyborgian future when he announces, 'I am lust personified,' before going on to explain, 'I am the first Gen-X rock-and-roll pornographer.' This is all in the context of his new album, *Slacker Jesus.* 'The front of the album is made out of a cross. When you look at a cross you usually think of Jesus bringing it down. But when you look at our cross it has television sets with nothing but power and lust. In the right-hand corner it says, 10.7.74, and that was the year I was born. And it has a little arrow here to the earth. You see, the year that Slacker Jesus was conceived on the earth.' Matt, who sports a Christ-like beard, has also had his hair streaked and straightened to more closely resemble the original Messiah.

'The album's saying that I am the rock-and-roll pornographer who has come down to lead the world and dominate it through lust and music. The Slacker Jesus is here to push you through into the next utopian society, a new society that's not gonna believe in monogamy, that's not gonna believe lesbianism shouldn't exist and that's gonna let you know that believing in your desire and letting it be your guide to life is OK.'

In reality, the Slacker Jesus is the son of the aforementioned Chuck Zane, who relocated his business, Zane Entertainment, to Porno Valley in the early 1990s. Matt Zane has had a video camera since he was seven. Having followed his father into the business, he has been directing porn films ever since he was twenty-one and in three years has directed over eighty. What makes him unusual is the way he is fusing porn and rock into a conceptual package. Of course sex and rock have always been entwined. 'In the old days it used to be a cool thing if a heavy metal band could get one of their dancing girls to flash their boobs. Now it's: "We've made a porn video of us backstage,"' says Doug Rushkoff. That is exactly what Matt Zane has done with *Sexual Society*, his latest film, a documentary following Zane on tour with his band, and fusing performance footage, backstage sex and tour-bus orgies: 'We have bondage, we have the band, we have strippers, we have live lesbian orgies, we've got booze, we've got piercing, we've got tattooing, we've got all that stuff.'

If there is such a thing, Matt Zane seems to be the living embodiment of Cronenberg's new flesh. 'It's gonna happen eventually, man. You can't keep lust down. Lust will always come up and it'll always come up and make you do crazy things. You can't deny lust and that's what I am. I am the physical manifestation of lust.' And yet in spite of all the hyperbole, there is something homely surrounding this zany rocker with a video camera for a gimmick.

'Kids have been jerking off to porn videos since they were sixteen and now that they're in their twenties they look at the porn video as a tool to use in their work, and their art,' says Doug Rushkoff. Perhaps it is really that simple. Looking out across Porno Valley, with its suburban streets, single-storey houses, front lawns, strip malls, business estates and warehouses, you would find it hard to believe that behind this vision of ordinary life, in the bedrooms and back yards of suburbia, dozens, and hundreds, of new porn videos are being made daily.

But that is the legacy of video. It has normalized pornography, taken away the taboo, the shame, the sense of transgression, and left in its place something as banal and commonplace as the cheap plastic shell of the video cassette itself.

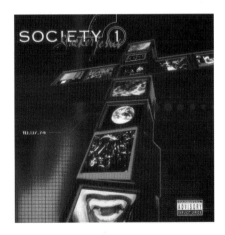

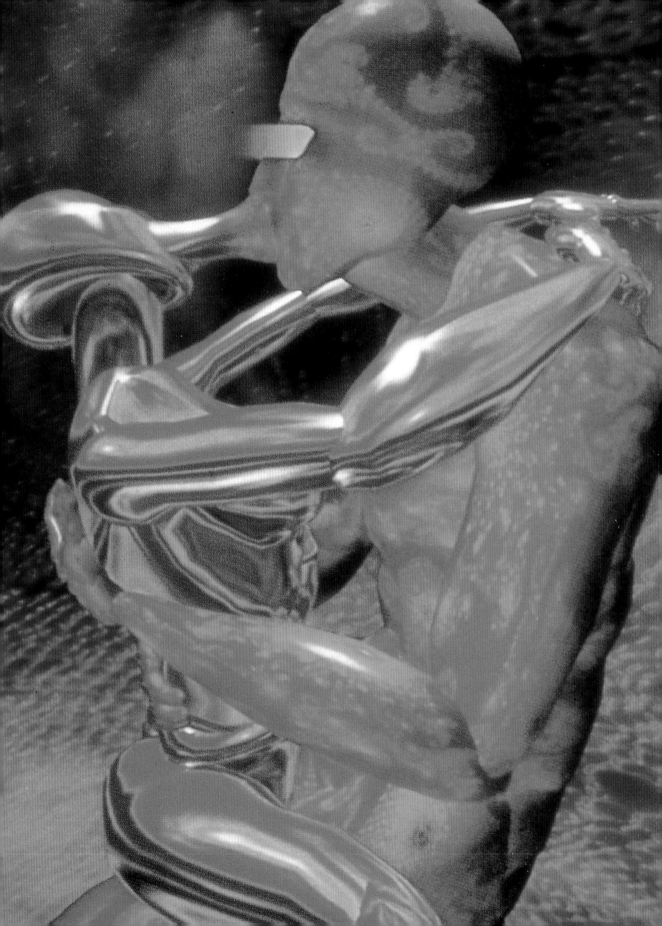

Pornotopia

[*Chapter Seven: Digital*]

I f the history of pornography can be told in terms of its technologies – print, photography, film, video – what of the future? Where print made sexual imagery more democratic (and consequently political), and photography made it real (and newly transgressive), and film made it a spectacle (in a new mass market), and video made it private (and more manipulable), the Internet and the new digital age have upped the pornographic ante. The democratic potential of older technologies is exponentially increased with a computer and a modem; images of spectacular bodies that were once the province of only the moneyed élite are now accessible to anyone – even, and most worryingly for some, children. The appeal of the 'real', first apparent in photography, is amplified by not only the images of real individuals but the potential to interact with them. The new choices afforded by video are far outstripped by a technology that allows near-infinite choice in the selection of images. As a medium that disseminates pornographic imagery, there is nothing that rivals the Internet's efficiency in catering for (and inevitably creating) specialist tastes. There are whole new sexual subcultures here, with virtual communities of fetishists, providing choice on an unprecedented scale.

The new technology is creating a new pornography, or pornographies, for the siliconed bleached blonde is now but one of many pornographic types. The uniformity imposed by the collective viewing of film, which was already being broken down with the advent of video, has disintegrated altogether on the Net. There are websites for people who fetishize women smoking, women lactating, coupling dwarves and amputees, bestiality with every possible species, pre-op, post-op and mid-op transsexuals – male to female, female to male: the list goes on. Mark Dery, author of *Escape Velocity*, says, 'There is no one so grotesquely Falstaffian, so hideously obese, so weirdly disfigured or malformed, that they can't be the subject of exploitation on the Internet. It's a democracy of exploitation.'[1]

◁ *Lawnmower Man* (1992): 'virtual reality' sex, as seen by Hollywood.

The Internet has increased the impression of aloneness while encouraging the illusion of intimacy. Chat rooms, newsgroups and bulletin boards (often called 'community sites' where people can 'meet', chat and share news) sprang up as quickly and quietly as the rest of the network. The pornographic newsgroups came in the first wave of an ocean currently made up of around 25,000 different groups, thousands of which appeal to a wide range of fetishes. As few of these fetishes have a large enough following to maintain a publication, the Internet, with its massive amount of free Web space, is an ideal forum. Those alone on the fringe have been sucked into their own specialized mainstream, and all the fish are biting.

With film you have to wait for your favourite bit; with video you can fast-forward and rewind. But with the Internet you can download, cut and paste those bits that are of interest only to you. When it comes to choice, the Internet is a world of instant gratification.

For the first time in history, pornography seems to have its own space – in the non-space that is cyberspace. Up until now pornography has always been homeless. It came into its own in the nineteenth century, at precisely the time when modern existence was beginning to be dominated by the two distinct categories of home and work. Pornography has no place in the home, but equally it has no place at work. Entry into either, being unsanctioned, is furtive – hidden in briefcases, under the bed. Pornography's marginal status has confined it to marginal spaces: red-light districts, the top shelf, adult cinemas. Not only are these places policed, but they allow access to pornography only as some kind of public transaction. The act of consumption is witnessed, the transgression is noted and the impression of shame is registered. The Internet, however, provides anonymity as perfect as you can get. There is no need to make a trip to the shop; in fact, there is no need for human contact at all. Internet browsers can be set up in such a way as to disallow information exchange between the computer and the webmaster so no details about visits to particular sites are recorded. This is the ultimate technology for consumers of pornography: no longer passive voyeurs – recipients of images presented by someone else – they can control what they see.

But with this new technology and its reconfigured pornographies comes anxiety. It is in our nature to be cautious about things we don't fully understand and so to look on them with suspicion. New technology, while interesting and useful, is frightening and engenders an atmosphere of mass caution, but with that also comes the potential for transgression and recklessness. The fear associated with these new media, including CD-ROM, DVD and the Internet, is complicated by the fact that fear of computing has been tightly woven into the fabric of our society since even before the introduction of the first workable mainframe. Add to this the bogey of pornography and you have a potent marriage ready to strike fear into the hearts of all upstanding citizens.

Late in 1995, an article was printed in the reputable US weekly news magazine *Time* about the prevalence of pornography on the Internet. At the centre of the story was a study by an electrical engineering student at Carnegie Mellon University named Marty Rimm. His study claimed that 83.5 per cent of the images on the

△ Computer screenshot of the Bad Kitty website: a combination of live video shows, stills, fan art, chat room, and branded merchandise. Sex delivered right to your desktop.

Usenet (a portion of the Internet which allows people to write and respond to messages on specialized topics) were pornographic. Rimm believed that 98.9 per cent of the consumers of on-line porn were men, and that there was evidence to suggest that the remaining 1.1 per cent of consumers were women who'd been paid to hang out in chat rooms to make the men feel more comfortable.[2] The cover of the issue was a digitally created image of a young child with a traumatized expression on his face peering at the screen of his computer, which in turned glowed greenly back at him. The methodology and statistics in the Rimm study were to be severely criticized in the following weeks, but it was already too late. Parents panicked. Anti-porn feminists kicked into high gear. Suddenly, it seemed, pornography was no longer confined to back alleys and top shelves. It was coming into our homes; it was coming to get us.

And it all started with the Soviet artificial satellite Sputnik in 1957. As the first Sputnik went up, the heads of American scientists dropped into their hands. They saw the launch as a sign of Soviet technical superiority. An argument about political and sociological principles had been taken to the skies and they were losing it.

The Soviets setting the pace was a clear indication to the USA not only that the Communist regime could survive, but also that it could prosper and perhaps even surpass the mighty American democracy, still optimistic and fresh from the relative success of Korea and not yet aware of the thorny green geography of Vietnam. To the defence department, the launch of Sputnik suggested a possibility that hadn't really taken hold of the popular imagination yet: nuclear war.

So it was that they started to work on creating an information network capable of surviving a nuclear holocaust. One Leonard Kleinhold at MIT first had the idea of sending packets of information through a multi-station network in the early 1960s. In 1969 there were four interconnected computers. By 1985 there were over 1,000 locations across the world with Internet capabilities. Four years later over 100,000 people were on-line and the first free server had been born. And just a little while after that the first hacker cracked the US Defense Department's security codes, thus giving the first inkling that perhaps the Internet wasn't so safe after all.

In the same way that printing was initially hailed by the Roman Catholic Church as a 'peaceful art', before it was realized that it had unexpected and unwelcome uses, so too the uses of the Internet exceeded all original expectations. What started out as a means to save the free world in extremis ended up distributing the world's porn – by the truckload. The most common words entered into search engines are sexually explicit. As the otherwise repressed consumer market has always known, sex sells. In the past it has always been used to sell other products, but now sex was selling itself. And people were buying it. The largest adult sites can get 1 million hits a day, far more than the site of a large company like General Electric might receive.

It is notoriously difficult to get reliable statistics on pornography on the Net but, according to one estimate, some 10,000 adult sites bring in a revenue of $1 billion a year, most of it through electronic credit-card transactions, some secure, some not so secure. A small adult site which gets 10,000 hits a day will typically gross about $3,000 a month. A medium-sized site with 50,000 hits a day can bring in about $20,000 a month. A particularly popular site with several million hits a day can typically bring in more than $1 million in a month.

But credit-card transactions aren't the only way to go. Free sites also make money by stocking their pages with click-though banners which result in pay-outs of 2 cents every time someone goes through. Many of these don't even have lewd contents but simply provide ad space. Sites such as these have been known to bring in as much as $1 million a year.[3]

The new technology is not just a vehicle for pornography; pornography may well be driving the technology. It's what Silicon Valley types call the 'killer', the engine that pulls the locomotive along. While there are no official figures, pornographic images coded in graphic formats like JPEG, GIF and streaming (real-time) video undoubtedly take up a large proportion of Web traffic. It is arguable, then, that pornography is, in part, driving the quest to shrink the file sizes on both pictures and video while increasing the resolution of the images. And it is reasonable to assume that pornography is significantly contributing to the demand for the Internet to be faster, more powerful, more reliable and more technologically sophisticated.

Predictably, the prospect of limitless pornographic images on-line for anyone who has a computer and a modem has prompted calls for action. Despite half a millennium of organized attempted censorship, pornographic transgressions have not been controlled, let alone eliminated. The Index for Print, the Paris Préfecture's regulation of the photographic image, the Obscene Publications Act, to name but three unrelated blunt instruments, merely serve to signpost the territory of increasing pornographic production. The futility of these mechanisms became ever more apparent as the twentieth century progressed. Prior to the Internet, there was a lively trade in illegal videos throughout the sex shops of Britain. There was always something futile about the routine busting of these sex shops, the viewing and logging of pornographic tapes, and the merry-go-round of confiscation and destruction through the magistrates' courts. But any attempt at censorship of the Internet takes this futility to an absurd level. The police are reduced to witnessing pornography – at their newly issued computers – rather than policing it. This is the ultimate picture of the censor as consumer. Anyone with a computer and a modem has access to the world's pornography; the police just add to the numbers. The Internet, existing outside real space, is not under the jurisdiction of any particular governing body. It is about as close as we are ever likely to get to organized anarchy. The game is up for the censors.

This does not stop people clamouring for something to be done. At the end of the millennium, calls for censorship are no longer raised in the name of women, the uneducated or the lower classes. This time, as with the hysteria generated by 'video nasties' in the 1980s, censorship is called for in the name of the child. This has the clear political advantage of being one of those rare areas in today's society that remain sacred. Everyone jumps to the call, and if they don't jump, at least they don't question (or at least not too loudly).

The calls for censorship, however, are hollow since the mechanisms of control are inadequate to the task. Pornography on-line, by some estimates, makes up to 20 per cent of the $4.5 billion made on-line in 1998. Regulation has proved difficult as jurisdiction is difficult to allocate. Small pockets of law enforcement have sprung up to try to regulate the problem, their success being just as small as their numbers. And for every porn distributor locked up a dozen more appear. Since 1995, according to one set of figures, the number of adult sites on-line has been increasing by 40 per cent every twelve months.[4]

If the game is up for the censors, why the need to pretend? It is anxiety that requires us to go through the rituals. According to Arthur C. Clarke, 'Any sufficiently advanced technology is indistinguishable from magic.' This is not the territory of rationality but of myth and magic and storytelling.

Porn started early on the Net, a phenomenon no doubt related to the fact that it is young men who take the keenest interest in the fresh new gismos and the pipe-dreams of new technology. A boy's toy, the Internet was used and programed and run by young men. It was the geek and not the meek who inherited the Net, a place which is for many people very much like the real world, just pixelated. Some of the earliest mailing lists – scheduled e-mail drops into multiple boxes – were of a pornographic nature, and **alt.binaries.pictures.erotica** was one of the very first newsgroups to be listed on

△▽ Leisure Suit Larry in his latest, sixth adventure, *Love for Sail!* One of the most enduring computer sex game characters, Larry's goal is to end up bedding as many women as he can. Which is usually not many.

the Usenet. But digital pictures, erotic or otherwise, can take up a lot of space. What was needed was a more powerful system to accommodate them. Modems got faster, bandwidths grew wider and, in the late 1980s, the first Internet browser, Mosaic, was introduced so you no longer even had to know where to look. You just had to ask the machine.

The sharp upturn in the evolution of the Internet follows a similar pattern to that of the computers it runs on. The early Net (ARPAnet), connecting a handful of university campuses, existed on super-computers the size of a large kitchen. The sophisticated Internet of today can run off a sturdy cellular phone. Today's computers are small, cheap and efficient, and despite the prediction of an IBM executive at the dawn of computing (he couldn't see any reason for there ever to be more than five computers in the entire world) everyone seems to either have one or be in the process of buying one.

The start of the 1980s saw the first computer sex games. One of the earliest was Soft Porn Adventure, which challenged players to bed as many women as they could. True to the format of the computer game, the last woman proved the greatest challenge, as she required a wedding ring on her finger before she would submit. The game was based on written descriptions of the scenario. Within a short time the graphics on home computers had improved enough to allow Soft Porn Adventure to turn into Leisure Suit Larry in the Land of the Lounge Lizards. Larry was then an eight-bit graphic with a square head and pointed knees. True to the original, his goal was seduction. This time Larry was a comic character who could be moved around rooms, chatting up women and getting it when he could (which wasn't often). And like the comic character he was, he spoke in balloons.

Not that Larry was the first digital character in a sex game. That privilege belongs to Custard's Last Stand, which featured the rape of young squaws – although Custard was not to stand for long, as he was soon banned. Next was MacPlaymate. This was a black-and-white drawing of a woman on a bed with a range of devices from dildos and feathers to a nurse's outfit to move on the action. The feminists who dubbed MacPlaymate 'MacRape' were not any happier with its CD-ROM successor, Virtual Valerie. Virtual Valerie was created by Mike Saenz, the artist behind MacPlaymate, and it rewarded players with images of sex with Valerie as long as they found the right things to say to her and the right buttons to push. If they failed, they got booted out of the apartment.

The CD-ROM was a technology well suited to pornography: small, robust, cheap to copy and able to store a lot of information. In 1994 20 per cent of the CD-ROM turnover was made up of pornography, which even then translated into $260 million in the US alone.[6] Again, the sheer size of the pornographic market suggests that the new technology is not simply a vehicle for but is driven by pornography. DVDs – Digital Versatile Discs – which give a laser-disc-quality picture and high-quality sound, are the new kids on the block. Unlike videotape, DVD allows you to jump to different points in the narrative, to see the action from different angles, or even see the out-takes. And DVD distributors claim that adult DVDs outnumber 'straight' films by a wide margin, with ten new ones going on sale every week.[7]

The world is moving fast and requires instant service. As Bernard Arcand points out, a society that can create fast food can create fast sex.[8] Technology delivers the instant gratification demanded. Anticipation is a thing of the past. Suddenly we don't have to work as hard or spend as much to get the pleasure we want.

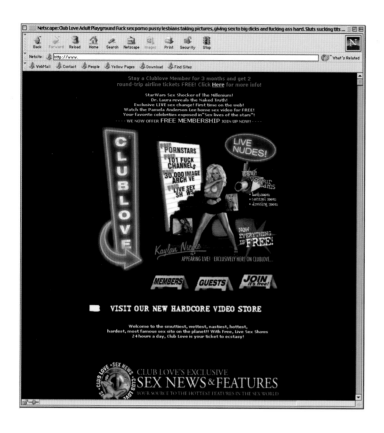

Netscape: Club Love Adult Playground Fuck sex porno pussy lesbians taking pictures, giving sex to big dicks and fucking ass hard. Sluts sucking tits ...

△▷ The extensive contents of the Club Love website, which includes live voyeur shows, audio, video and stills archive, and, for those looking for interaction, live chat with one-way video. Something for everyone?

For many, this picture has limited appeal. Pornography and the Internet provoke a peculiar marriage of anxieties. If individually each contributes to the increasing atomization of society, perhaps the fear is that together they represent its disintegration: the increasing individualism, the rupturing of extended family ties in favour of the nuclear family. 'In a society the size of Copenhagen, the municipal police gathered during the year something like seven or eight thousand dead bodies. People who died alone in their apartments,' says Bernard Arcand. 'It's a corollary of the fact that we live more and more alone.'[9] A study by Mintel reveals that there are more than 7 million people living alone in the UK and that total is expected to increase to 8.28 million by 2003 – one in three of all households.

People alone in their rooms, connected to the outside world via a machine and getting aroused by signs on a computer screen – some have seen in this a microcosm of an alienated society in which individuals are no longer relating to each other on a human level. Arcand talks of 'cocoons of individuals who have a good time with themselves thinking that they are relating to the rest of the world'.

Perhaps this 'deliriously disengaged guilt-free sex on-line that doesn't leave a sticky trail behind it' shouldn't surprise us in a post-AIDS world. As Mark Dery says, 'There's little wonder that the fantasy of discorporate guilt-free sex without secretions and some sort of neo-platonic world on the other side of the cathode-ray screen should be a seductive alternative at a moment when mating rituals and singles bars are fraught with fears about socially transmitted diseases.'[10]

What the Internet gives is the potential to be the ultimate voyeur. It promises that you will not be caught looking, if you don't want to be. It is the ultimate in dissociation from the object of interest. It is, as Dery would say, the 'Norman Bates' moment, where peering through peepholes is preferable to engagement. The only difference is that where Norman Bates was a specimen of psychopathology, voyeurism and disengagement on the Internet are becoming increasingly ordinary. This detachment from reality has not always been so readily tolerated. As Arcand says, 'You can lose yourself in a world of illusion which becomes your experience of reality. Traditionally we considered that form of behaviour pathological, and we took care of these people. What is happening is possibly that technology makes that form of behaviour more and more possible, more and more acceptable, or at least less and less disturbing for the rest of the population.'[11]

But if the new digital age has its detractors, it also has its exponents. Sex on-line does not scare everybody. As journalist Susannah Breslin says, 'To me, all sex is masturbatory. And if two people are having sex, and the woman masturbates in order to get off, does that mean it's not sex? Or does that mean that she just masturbated? And the only difference between that and two people in a chat room is that the people actually having physical sex are in the same room, and the other two people aren't. And that seems irrelevant; an unnecessary real-world thing.'[12]

Cyber-sex may not be sex as we know it, but for some it is about a new kind of human connection. It is much more about intimacy for those who are, for whatever reason, not currently prepared for physical intimacy or feel incapable of pursuing it. It takes the body out of the equation, and with it go the ways in which the physical can influence the trajectory of relationships. Cyber-sex is an abstract experience which to some can be more intimate than traditional relationships.

Chat rooms are the key to sex on the Internet. This is very much the aspect of the Net we are most dubious about. Chatting is all done on-line and in little soundbites – you won't get more than a sentence in at a time, and to avoid confused strands you have to type fast and be ready with abbreviations. Chat rooms have become very much a part of porn lore and myth and are held to be a prime meeting place for paedophiles and their prey. It's easy to get into a chat room and even easier to get out, and you are, more than anywhere else on the Net, safely anonymous. However, you can't lurk in a chat room unnoticed. Everyone else in that room knows you're there. You can duck into a private chat room if you want to chat with an individual, and this is perhaps where people get nervous. But, as with the Internet in general, it is compulsive and it strips inhibitions. Existing in a netherworld between pornography and sex, chat rooms are what we often think of when we consider sex on-line.

△ Slow, grainy (but live) video feeds from cameras placed in women's bedrooms. Much Web traffic is taken up by such information-heavy images.

▷ *Future Sex* magazine had an ambitious vision of sex on the Net: real-time physical interaction through the (non-existent) technology of teledildonics. Part of the hype that goes with the territory.

What exactly *is* sex on-line? Former editor of *Future Sex* magazine, Lisa Palac, recounts the first time she 'went private' with someone she calls GI Joe:

Once we were alone, GI said he wanted us to 'get to know' each other. I wanted to get off but saw no reason for the two to be mutually exclusive. I talked about how I enjoyed going to strip joints and throwing money down. He'd never heard of a woman who did that. I talked about the kinds of porn I liked to watch. He'd never heard of a woman who did that either. I assumed my unusual interests were wowing him, so I cut to the chase and told him to unzip his pants and grab his cock. In all caps he responded, WHAT ARE YOU, SOME KIND OF FAGGOT? And then he disappeared for ever.

Not all sex on-line is so *interruptus*. Palac then struck up an on-line relationship with 'Stephen Hadley': 'It happened five years ago. I met him on-line. His name was Stephen. We chatted for a few hours in real time and then the conversation quickly turned to sex. I asked him for his phone number because I thought, well, it's better that I call him in case he's really a psychopath masquerading as a normal person. We had phone sex that evening, and by the end of the night I felt that this was some of the most incredible sex that I had ever had in my life, even though I had physically never been in the same room with this man – we weren't even on the same coast. It was pretty amazing.

'Our relationship continued like this, on-line, for several weeks, and I finally said, "Look, I need to meet you." And he was really resistant and sort of shrugged it off, and I thought initially that maybe I had been tricked, that he was one of the cyber cads who try to trick women and get free sex on-line. Eventually, he confessed to me that he was really ashamed to meet me because he was very overweight, and I jokingly said, "Oh, come on, we all think we're too fat", but he was 350 pounds. And at that point it really didn't matter to me because I felt like I was in love with him, our sexual connection was so strong. I suddenly got the idea that I could meet him blindfolded and that would still be a way for us to keep a sense of the virtual relationship alive. So I flew to New York on my thirtieth birthday, and I was blindfolded and we made love, and when it was all over the plan was that I would just be whisked away in a taxi cab, and I wouldn't actually see

UTURE
Sex
ISSUE ▸ 2

CYBERSEX
STRAP IN, TWEAK OUT, TURN ON!

SMART APHRODISIACS

Voyeurism IN
Black & White

$4.95 / Canada $5.95

a Dick Thing ● Degradation for Hire ●The Latest in Erotic Entertainmel

△▽ Seymour Butts, a game fulfilling the couch potato's dream: chat up women who then take their clothes off – without leaving your sofa.

what he looked like. But after you have that kind of experience with someone, whatever it is, you have to know, and so I took the blindfold off, and I just thought he was the most beautiful man that I had ever seen. It was really magical.'[14]

The technology – as technology always does – has created a new experience, provided a novel perspective on the world, and a novel way of interacting with it. Palac's experience wasn't about an alternative reality; it was real and odd in what is now a fantastically ordinary way. For her and for others, the technology is reconfiguring human relationships. Some might even call them 'post-human'. The term 'post-human' is one that has arisen in the last few decades. Less frequently used than 'post-modern', it is about as well understood. Post-human deals with concepts based around the idea that our evolution is just as motivated by technology as it is by biology. In this sense any relationships we strike up on the Internet, particularly and maybe even especially sexual relationships, could be considered post-human.

One of the many fears prompted by the existence of pornography on the Internet is that it can invade our homes; that it marks an acceptance of pornography in our

everyday lives – part of a larger process we have already seen on TV and in magazines. But if pornography becomes an everyday event, will it still be transgressive, and if not, will it still be pornography? Will the great Victorian experiment that locked lewd artefacts away and labelled them 'pornography' be seen as an historical aberration, or are we now walled up in the secret museum for good? If one of the problems of trying to tell our history is that the concepts we use are the products of the very processes we seek to understand, what hope of telling our future? As pornography is but one aspect of the increasing individualism, atomization, compartmentalization and extremism that characterizes much of our lives – from sex to food, from work to play – we have no more reason to think that it will disappear, or at least disappear more quickly, than they will. If pornography does change, however (and already the new technologies are reconfiguring its contours), one thing remains certain: whatever pornography we get will be the pornography we deserve.

Notes

Unless otherwise indicated, an author's name and page reference are given below, and the full reference for the relevant title appears in the Select Bibliography. (Where the Select Bibliography contains more than one title by the same author, or more than one author with the same surname, the date of publication is also given.)

Introduction

1. Hebditch and Anning.
2. Webb.
3. Kendrick.
4. Williams.
5. Arcand.
6. Hunt (1993).
7. James Atlas, 'The Loose Canon', in *The New Yorker*, 29 March 1999, pp. 60–5.
8. Kendrick, p. 6.

Chapter One

1. Arcand (1993), pp. 125, 126.
2. Kendrick; also noted in Wagner (1988).
3. Kendrick, p. 11, and Andrew Wallace-Hadrill in interview for Channel 4 series.
4. Quoted in Grant and Mulas, pp. 18, 23.
5. Interview for Channel 4 series.
6. Andrew Wallace-Hadrill, 'Under the Sign of the Goat', in *The Times Literary Supplement*, 12 June 1998.
7. Quoted in Rattray Taylor, p. 209.
8. In Marryat, p. 274.
9. Charles Warne, quoted in Castleden, p. 17.

10. Castleden explores these possibilities in *The Cerne Giant*.
11. Grinsell documents the development of these Cerne Abbas Giant illustrations in 'The Cerne Abbas Giant: 1764–1980', pp. 29–33.
12. Quoted in Castleden.
13. Interview for Channel 4 series.
14. Kendrick first argued for the symbolic significance of the secret museum in establishing the category 'pornography'. For more on the history of the collection, see Antonio de Simone, 'The History of the Museum and the Collection', in Grant and Mulas, pp. 1–32.
15. Discussed by Nead in Douzinas and Nead (1999), and in Nead (1992), p. 25.
16. Quoted in Marcus, p. 19.
17. *L'Onanism*, 6th ed. (Lausanne, 1775), p. 60.
18. M. L. Barré, *Herculanum et Pompéi: Receuil général des peintures, bronzes, mosaïques, etc.*, 8 vols., quoted in Kendrick, p. 15.
19. Examples given in Clarke, pp. 206–12.
20. Clarke, p. 178.
21. Interview for Channel 4 series.
22. Quoted in Kendrick, p. 8.
23. Quoted in Rugoff.
24. Gay, vol. 1, p. 467.
25. These statistics appear in Clarke, p. 195.
26. Interview for Channel 4 series.
27. Clarke, pp. 212–40; see also Jacobelli, pp. 61, 65, 92–7.
28. Interview for Channel 4 series.
29. Johns, p. 11.
30. Johns, p. 30.

Chapter Two

1. St Augustine, *De Continentia*, quoted in Weir and Jerman, p. 83.
2. St Augustine, *Confessions* (second book), quoted in Weir and Jerman, p. 83.
3. St Augustine, *City of God*, quoted in Miles, p. 94.
4. For further reading on St Augustine, see Brown (1988).
5. 1 Corinthians vii: 1.
6. Matthew xix: 12.
7. For these and other examples, see Rouselle, p. 152.
8. Pachomius, *Precepts*, 2, quoted in Rouselle, p. 155.
9. Discussed by Constable, p. 208.
10. See Brundage (1996), p. 36. See also Brundage (1987), pp. 319–23, 481–5, 544–6.
11. Brundage (1996), p. 42.
12. Johns, p. 113.
13. Foucault, p. 21.
14. Paolo Segneri, *L'instruction de pénitent* (French trans. 1695, p. 301), quoted in Foucault, p. 20.
15. Foucault, p. 19.
16. Gerald of Wales, *The Jewel of the Church*, ed. J. T. Hagen, quoted in Camille (1992), p. 73.
17. Quoted in Cohn, p. 135.
18. Peter of Celle, quoted in Camille (1992), p. 65.
19. Weir and Jerman, p. 11.
20. Weir and Jerman, p. 14.
21. Weir and Jerman.
22. Weir and Jerman argue this position; see also Andersen.
23. Interview for Channel 4 series.
24. Episodes recounted in Rouselle, p. 152.
25. Interview for Channel 4 series.
26. Interview for Channel 4 series.
27. Interview for Channel 4 series.
28. Eusebius, vol. 1, p. 268.
29. Story in Freedburg, p. 322.
30. Paula Findlen, 'Humanism, Politics and Pornography in Renaissance Italy', in Hunt (1993), p. 57.
31. Quoted in Mancinelli.
32. Mancinelli.
33. Quoted in Webb.
34. Mancinelli.
35. Interview for Channel 4 series.
36. Quoted in Freedburg, p. 345.
37. Interview for Channel 4 series.
38. Interview for Channel 4 series.
39. Webb has already used these two paintings to make a similar point, pp.108–9.

Chapter Three

1. See, for instance, McLuhan (1962), and McLuhan (1964).
2. Quoted in Eisenstein, p. 148.
3. Eisenstein.
4. Febvre and Martin, p. 191.
5. Febvre and Martin, p. 317.
6. Febvre and Martin, p. 310.
7. Hyde, p. 65.
8. Boccaccio, p. 658.
9. Boccaccio, p. 277.
10. See Hyde, p. 71.
11. Berger, p. 7.
12. See Ginzburg, p. 77.
13. Quoted in Brown (1987), p. 241.
14. Freedburg, p. 361.
15. Freedburg, p. 362.
16. Freedburg, p. 368.
17. Arcand, p. 130.
18. Vasari, vol. 6, pp. 104–5.
19. Interview for Channel 4 series.
20. Ludovico Dolce, quoted in Paula Findlen (see note 2.30), in Hunt (1993), p. 108.
21. Interview for Channel 4 series.
22. Vasari.
23. Scheiner's translation, p. 20.
24. Scheiner, pp. 17–18.
25. Pietro Aretino, quoted in Webb, p. 347, and Kendrick, p. 59.
26. Pietro Aretino, quoted in Lawner, p. 14.
27. Pietro Aretino, 'Ragionamenti', quoted in Paula Findlen (see note 2.30), in Hunt (1993), p. 77.
28. Interview for Channel 4 series.

29. Kendrick.
30. Pepys, entries 8, 9 February, vol. 9, pp. 57–9. See also Webb, p. 347, and Scheiner, p. 14.
31. Kendrick, p. 62.
32. See Kendrick and Webb for more examples. For a full account of the Aretino story, see Talvacchia.
33. Quoted in Lynn Hunt, 'Obscenity and the Origins of Modernity', in Hunt (1993), p. 20.
34. Hunt (1993), p. 301.
35. For these and other examples, see Hunt, 'Pornography and the French Revolution', in Hunt (1993), pp. 301–39.
36. Hunt (1993).

Chapter Four

1. Clark, pp. 3–4.
2. For a discussion of the naked–nude dichotomy, see Nead.
3. Scharf, p. 140.
4. For details of Darnay's case, see McCauley, p. 157.
5. Scharf, p. 345.
6. Report of the Commission of the Chamber of Deputies, presented by M. Arago, Deputy for Pyrénées-Orientales, 3 July 1839, quoted in Trachtenberg, p. 19.
7. Quoted in Langford, pp. 5, 6.
8. Trachtenberg, p. 4.
9. Edgar Allan Poe, *Alexander's Weekly Magazine*, 15 January 1840, quoted in Trachtenberg, p. 37.
10. For discussion of the significance of Pliny's story, see Bryson.
11. Quoted in Scharf, p. 139.
12. Interview for Channel 4 series.
13. Romer, in his foreword to *Die Erotische Daguerreotypie*.
14. Interview for Channel 4 series.
15. Charles Baudelaire, *The Modern Public and Photography*, quoted in Trachtenberg, p. 87.
16. Louis Veuillot, *Les Odeurs de Paris* (1867), quoted in McCauley, p. 183.
17. McCauley, p. 183.
18. Quoted in Romer (see note 4.13).
19. Barthes, p. 3.
20. Barthes, p. 82.
21. Solomon-Godeau, pp. 232–3.
22. Walter Benjamin quoted in Trachtenberg, p. 202.
23. Quoted in Scharf, p. 130.
24. Gabriel Pelin, *Les Laideurs du Beau Paris* (1861), quoted in McCauley, p. 156.
25. Quoted in McCauley, p. 158.
26. Lady Elizabeth Eastlake, 'Photography', *London Quarterly Review*, March 1857, quoted in Trachtenberg, pp. 40, 41.
27. McCauley, pp. 157–60.
28. *The Times*, 20 April 1874.
29. Dr Bill Thompson of Reading University in interview for Channel 4 series.
30. Solomon-Godeau, p. 233.
31. Interview for Channel 4 series.
32. Quoted in Gabor, p. 41.
33. This order of progression is pointed out by Gabor, pp. 76–80.
34. Gabriel Pelin (see note 4.24), quoted in McCauley, p. 158.
35. Interview for Channel 4 series.
36. Interview for Channel 4 series.
37. Interview for Channel 4 series.
38. Interview for Channel 4 series.

Chapter Five

1. Quoted in Dewe Mathews, p. 9.
2. Linda Williams gives a ground-breaking analysis of the development of pornography, using Muybridge, Foucault and the concept of 'the frenzy of the visible' in her classic book, *Hard Core: Power, Pleasure and the 'Frenzy of the Visible'*, pp. 1–57.
3. Quoted in Williams, p. 52.
4. Linda Williams in interview for Channel 4 series.
5. Interview for Channel 4 series.
6. Berger, p. 47.
7. See Williams.
8. Walter Serener, 'Kino und Schaulust', *Die Schaubühne*, 9 (1913), quoted in Kaes, pp 53–4.

9. Interview for Channel 4 series.

10. Interview for Channel 4 series.

11. Quoted in Gertrude Koch, 'The Body's Shadow Realm', in *October*, No. 50, p. 4.

12. For these and other examples of blue movies or 'stags', see Di Lauro and Rabkin.

13. Marcus, p. 273.

14. Williams, p. 63.

15. Example given in Mathews, p. 35.

16. O'Toole, p. 65.

17. Di Lauro and Rabkin, p. 52.

18. Quoted in Mathews, pp. 152, 153.

19. Interview for Channel 4 series.

20. Interview for Channel 4 series.

21. Interview for Channel 4 series.

22. Hebditch and Anning, p. 225.

Chapter Six

1. RCA press release, 10 September 1969.

2. Statistics from CEMA Research Centre.

3. See Williams.

Chapter Seven

1. Interview for Channel 4 series.

2. Philip Elmer-DeWitt, 'On a Screen Near You: Cyberporn', in *Time* magazine, 3 July 1995.

3. Randy Barrett, 'Porn Pays Big Time Online', in *InterActive Week Online*, 29 October 1997.

4. *Broadcasting Cable Online*, 5 November 1998.

5. Interview for Channel 4 series. See also Mark Bennett, 'Digital Kinks', in *Skin Two*, issue 12.

6. Maxwell, p. 252.

7. Andy Riga, 'Virtual Sex Industry Panting for Faster Internet Delivery: New Technology is Being Driven by the Porn Market', in *The Ottowa Citizen*, 26 November 1998.

8. Interview for Channel 4 series.

9. Interview for Channel 4 series.

10. Interview for Channel 4 series.

11. Interview for Channel 4 series.

12. Interview for Channel 4 series.

13. Palac, p. 104.

14. Interview for Channel 4 series.

Select Bibliography

Individual essays are cross-referred to the relevant anthology.

J. Andersen, *The Witch on the Wall* (Allen & Unwin; London, 1977).

Bernard Arcand, *The Jaguar and the Anteater: Pornography Degree Zero* (Verso; London, 1993).

Antoine de Baecque, 'Pamphlets: Libel and Political Mythology' in *Revolution in Print: The Press in France*, eds. Robert Darnton and Daniel Roche (University of California Press and the New York Public Library; Berkeley, 1989).

Roland Barthes, *Camera Lucida* (Vintage; London, 1993).

Walter Benjamin, *Illuminations* (Cape; London, 1970).

John Berger, *Ways of Seeing* (Penguin; Harmondsworth, 1972).

Giovanni Boccaccio, *The Decameron*, trans. G. H. McWilliam (Penguin; Harmondsworth, 1995).

D. Catherine Brown, *Pastor and Laity in the Theology of Jean Gerson* (Cambridge University Press; Cambridge, 1987).

Peter Brown, *The Body and Society: Men, Women, and Sexual Renunciation in Early Christianity* (Columbia University; New York, 1988).

James A. Brundage, *Law, Sex and Christian Society in Medieval Europe* (University of Chicago Press; Chicago, 1987).

James A. Brundage, 'Sex and Canon Law', in *Handbook of Medieval Sexuality*, ed. Vern L. Bullough and James A. Brundage (Garland Publishing; New York, 1996).

Norman Bryson, *Vision and Painting: The Logic of the Gaze* (Macmillan; London, 1983).

Michael Camille, *The Gothic Idol: Ideology and Image-making in Medieval Art* (Cambridge University Press; Cambridge, 1989).

Michael Camille, *Image on the Edge: The Margins of Medieval Art* (Reaktion; London, 1992).

Michael Camille, 'Obscenity Under Erasure: Censorship in Medieval Illuminated Manuscripts', in *Obscenity, Social Control and Artistic Creation in the European Middle Ages* (Brill; Boston/Leiden, 1998).

Rodney Castleden, *The Cerne Giant* (Dorset Publishing; Wincanton, 1996).

Pamela Church Gibson and Roma Gibson, *Dirty Looks: Women. Pornography. Power.* (BFI Publishing; London, 1993).

Kenneth Clark, *The Nude* (Penguin; London, 1985).

John R. Clarke, *Looking at Lovemaking: Constructions of Sexuality in Roman Art 100 BC–AD 250* (University of California Press; Berkeley, 1998).

Norman Cohn, *Europe's Inner Demons: The Demonization of Christians in Medieval Christendom* (Pimlico; London, 1993).

Jean-Louis Comolli, 'Machines of the Visible', in *The Cinematic Apparatus*, eds. Teresa de Lauretis and Stephen Heath (St Martin's Press; New York, 1980).

Giles Constable, 'Aelred of Rievaulx and the Nun of Watton: An Episode in the Early History of the Gilbertine Order', in *Medieval Women*, ed. Derek Baker (Basil Blackwell; Oxford, 1978).

Mark Dery, *Escape Velocity: Cyberculture at the End of the Century* (Grove Press; New York, 1996).

Tom Dewe Mathews, *Censored!* (Chatto & Windus; London, 1994).

Al Di Lauro and Gerald Rabkin, *Dirty Movies: An Illustrated History of the Stag Film, 1915–1970* (Chelsea House; London, 1976).

C. Douzinas and L. Nead (eds.), *Law and the Image: The Authority of Art and the Aesthetics of Law* (University of Chicago Press; Chicago, 1999).

Elizabeth L. Eisenstein, *The Printing Revolution in Early Modern Europe* (Cambridge University Press; Cambridge, 1983).

Eusebius, *The Ecclesiastical History and the Martyrs of Palestine*, trans. Hugh Jackson Lawlor and John Ernest Oulton (Society for Promoting Christian Knowledge; New York and Toronto, 1927), vol. 1.

Lucien Febvre, Henri-Jean Martin, *The Coming of the Book: The Impact of Printing, 1450–1800* (Verso; London, 1976).

Michel Foucault, vol. 1, 'The Will to Knowledge', in *The History of Sexuality* (Penguin; Harmondsworth, 1981).

David Freedburg, *The Power of Images* (University of Chicago Press; Chicago, 1989).

Peter Fryer, *Private Case, Public Scandal* (Secker & Warburg; London, 1966).

Mark Gabor, *The Pin Up: A Modest History* (Universe Books; New York, 1972).

Peter Gay, 'The Bourgeois Experience: Victoria to Freud', in *Education of the Senses* (Oxford University Press; New York, 1987), vol. 1.

Carlo Ginzburg, 'Titian, Ovid and Sixteenth Century Codes for Erotic Illustration', in *Myths, Emblems, Clues* (Hutchinson Radius; London, 1990).

Michael Grant and Antonia Mulas, *Eros in Pompeii: The Erotic Art Collection of the Museum of Naples* (Stewart, Tabori & Chang; New York, 1997).

Leslie Grinsell, 'The Cerne Abbas Giant: 1764–1980', in *Antiquity*, No. 54, 1980.

David Hebditch and Nick Anning, *Porn Gold* (Faber & Faber; London, 1988).

Lynn Hunt, *Eroticism and the Body Politic* (Johns Hopkins University Press; Baltimore, 1991).

Lynn Hunt (ed.), *The Invention of Pornography: Obscenity and the Origins of Modernity, 1500–1800* (Zone Books; New York, 1993).

Annette Kuhn, *Cinema, Censorship and Sexuality 1909–1925* (Routledge; London, 1988).

H. Montgomery Hyde, *A History of Pornography* (Heinemann; London, 1964).

Luciana Jacobelli, *Le Pitture Erotiche delle Terme Suburbane di Pompeii* ('L'Erma' di Bretschneider; Rome, 1995).

Catherine Johns, *Sex or Symbol? Erotic Images of Greece and Rome* (British Museum Press; London, 1982).

Jane Juffer, *At Home with Pornography: Women, Sex and Everyday Life* (New York; London, 1998).

Anton Kaes (ed.), *Kino-Debatte* (Deutscher Taschenbuch; Munich, 1978).

Walter Kendrick, *The Secret Museum: Pornography in Modern Culture* (University of California Press; Berkeley, 1987).

Michael Langford, *The Story of Photography: From its Beginnings to the Present Day* (Focal Press; Oxford, 1997).

Robin Lane Fox, *Pagans and Christians in the Mediterranean World from the Second Century AD to the Conversion of Constantine* (Penguin; London, 1988).

Lynne Lawner, *I Modi: The Sixteen Pleasures, An Erotic Album of the Italian Renaissance* (Owen; London, 1988).

Edward Lucie-Smith, *Sexuality in Western Art* (Thames & Hudson; London, 1991).

Fabrizio Mancinelli, 'Michelangelo's *Last Judgement*: Technique and Restoration', in *Michelangelo – The Last Judgement: A Glorious Restoration* (Harry N. Abrams; New York, 1997).

Steven Marcus, *The Other Victorians* (Basic Books; New York, 1966).

Frederick Marryat, *A Diary in America With Remarks on Its Institutions* (first published 1839), ed. Sydney Jackman (Knopf; New York, 1962), 2 vols.

Kenneth Maxwell, *A Sexual Odyssey: From Forbidden Fruit to Cybersex* (Plenum Press; New York, 1996).

Iain McCalman, *Radical Underworld: Prophets, Revolutionaries and Pornographers in London, 1795–1840* (Cambridge University Press; Cambridge, 1988).

Elizabeth Anne McCauley, *Industrial Madness: Commercial Photography in Paris 1848–1871* (Yale University Press; New Haven, 1994).

Marshall McLuhan, *The Gutenberg Galaxy: The Making of Typographic Man* (Routledge & Kegan Paul; London, 1962).

Marshall McLuhan, *Understanding Media: The Extensions of Man* (McGraw-Hill; New York, 1964).

Margaret R. Miles, *Carnal Knowing: Female Nakedness and Religious Meaning in the Christian West* (Burns & Oates; Tunbridge Wells, 1992).

Laura Mulvey, *Visual and Other Pleasures* (Macmillan; London, 1989).

Serge Nazarieff, *Early Erotic Photography* (Taschen; Cologne, 1993).

Lynda Nead, *The Female Nude: Art, Obscenity and Sexuality* (Routledge; London, 1992).

Gilles Néret, *Erotica Universalis* (Tachen; Cologne, 1994).

Beaumont Newhall, *The History of Photography* (The Museum of Modern Art; New York, 1982).

Laurence O'Toole, *Pornocopia: Porn, Sex, Technology and Desire* (Serpent's Tail; London, 1998).

Lisa Palac, *The Edge of the Bed: How Dirty Pictures Changed My Life* (Little, Brown; Boston, 1998).

Jean-Jacques Pauvert, *Estampes Erotiques Révolutionnaires* (Henri Veyrier; Paris, 1989).

Samuel Pepys, *The Diary of Samuel Pepys*, eds. Robert Latham and William Matthews, II vols. (University of California; Berkeley, 1970–83).

Baxter Phillips, *Cut: The Unseen Cinema* (Bounty Books; New York, 1975).

Amy Richlin, *The Garden of Priapus: Sexuality and Aggression in Roman Humor* (Yale University Press; New Haven, London, 1983).

Amy Richlin (ed.), *Pornography and Representations in Greece and Rome* (Oxford University Press; Oxford, 1992).

Jill M. Ricketts, *Visualizing Boccaccio: Studies and Illustrations of the Decameron from Giotto to Pasolini* (Cambridge University Press; Cambridge, 1997).

Grant B. Romer, *Die Erotische Daguerreotypie*, ed. Rainer Wick (Weingarten; Freiberg, 1989).

Aline Rouselle, *Porneia: On Desire and the Body in Antiquity* (Basil Blackwell; Oxford, 1988).

Milton Rugoff, *Prudery and Passion* (Rupert Hart-Davis; London, 1972).

Aaron Scharf, *Art and Photography* (Penguin; Harmondsworth, 1983).

Uwe Scheid Collection, *1,000 Nudes* (Taschen; Cologne, 1994).

Clifford J. Scheiner, *The Essential Guide to Erotic Literature: Part One* (Wordsworth Editions; London, 1996).

Abigail Solomon-Godeau, 'Reconsidering Erotic Photography', in *Photography at the Dock: Essays on Photographic History, Institutions and Practices* (University of Minnesota Press; Minneapolis, 1991).

Susan Sontag, *On Photography* (Penguin; London, 1979).

Bette Talvacchia, *Taking Positions: On the Erotic in Renaissance Culture* (Princeton University Press; Princeton, 1999).

G. Rattray Taylor, *Sex in History* (Thames & Hudson; London, 1953).

Roger Thompson, *Unfit for Modest Ears: A Study of Pornographic, Obscene and Bawdy Works Written or Published in England in the Second Half of the Seventeenth Century* (Macmillan; London, 1979).

Alan Trachtenberg (ed.), *Classic Essays on Photography* (Leete's Island Books; New Haven, 1980).

Giorgio Vasari, *Lives of the Most Eminent Painters, Sculptors and Architects*, trans. Gaston daC. de Vere (Macmillan and the Medici Society, London, 1912–15), vol. 6.

Peter Wagner, *Eros Revived: Erotica of the Enlightenment in England and America* (Secker & Warburg; London, 1988).

Peter Wagner, *Erotica and the Enlightenment* (P. Lang; Frankfurt and New York, 1991).

Peter Wagner, 'Obscenity and Body Language in the French Revolution', in *Reading Iconotexts: From Swift to the French Revolution* (Reaktion; London, 1995).

Andrew Wallace-Hadrill, *Houses and Society in Pompeii and Herculaneum* (Princeton University Press; Princeton, 1994).

Peter Webb, *The Erotic Arts* (Secker & Warburg; London, 1975).

Anthony Weir and James Jerman, *Images of Lust: Sexual Carvings on Medieval Churches* (B. T. Batsford; London, 1986).

Linda Williams, *Hard Core: Power, Pleasure and the 'Frenzy of the Visible'* (Pandora; London, 1990; first published in the USA 1989).

Picture Acknowledgements

AKG London: 17 (Jean Louis Nou), 44, 49, 60, 67, 69 (Erich Lessing), 70 top right (S. Domingie/ M.Rabatti), 77, 96 (Erich Lessing), 116 top (Erich Lessing)

Alinari Fratelli: 39, 62, 70 top left

Ashmolean Museum, Oxford: 43

Bad Kitty: 169

Bastion Public Relations: 172–3

Bibliotheque Nationale de France: 90 bottom, 91, 92 top, 99, 101

Bridgeman Art Library/Duke of Sutherland Collection/National Gallery of Scotland: 97 right

Bildarchiv Foto Marburg: 53 bottom

British Library: 30, 31 top and bottom, 32, left, 93

British Museum: 51, 38, 72, 78, 79 top and bottom, 83, 84 top and bottom

Colorific!/Shooting Star: 134, 133, 135 bottom, 135 top (J.R. Collection), 137, 138

Corbis/Everett: 136

David Sarnoff Collection: 144, 145

Ettore Castellano: 132

Evil Angel Productions: 161, 162–3

Fortean Picture Library: 28

Fortean Picture/Janet and Colin Bord Library: 52

Fotomas Index (UK): 76

Future Sex™ magazine/Bill Weiss: 177

Homegrown Video: 158

Home Video magazine: 146

Hot d'Or: 149 top, 151 bottom

Hulton Getty Picture Collection: 120 bottom, 120–1 top

Huntley Film Archives: 119

Internet Entertainment Group/Club Love.com: 174, 175, 176

Kinsey Institute for Research in Sex, Gender and Reproduction, Inc.: 90 top, 124, 125, 126, 127, 128, 129

Klinger Collection: 87

Kobal Collection: 10 (Sidney Baldwin), 12 bottom, 12 top (G. Lefkowitz/New Line)

Michael Larvey: 32 right, 36 bottom, 36 top,

MacQuitty International Collection: 56 top

Mark Gabor: 113, 114 right, 114 left, 115 top

Metro Home Video: 154, 155

Antonia Mulas: 15, 22, 24, 25 top, 26, 33, 34, 40, 42

National Gallery, London: 68, 81 bottom

New Machine Publishing Inc.: 178–9

Oeffentliche Kunstsammlung Basel, Kunstmuseum/Martin Buhler: 54

Penthouse Photographs, General Media Communications Inc.: 115 bottom, 117 top left

Photo Scala, Florence: 41, 55, 61, 63, 64, 65, 66, 71 bottom, 71 top, 82

Pierpont Morgan Library, New York: 57, 58, 59

Prefecture de Police: 97 left, 110

Private: 148

Ken Probst: 14, 18, 142, 152

Reunion des Musée Nationaux/J.G. Berizzi: 81 top

Ronald Grant Archive: 8, 118, 123, 130, 139, 140, 141, 166

Clifford J. Scheiner: 86

Societé Francaise de Photographie: 100

Solo Syndication / Daily Mail, courtesy of the Centre for the Study of Cartoons and Caricature, University of Kent, Canterbury: 48

Totally Tasteless Video: 156, 157

Universal City Studios Licensing Inc.: 164

George Urban: 160 bottom

Uwe Scheid Collection: 20, 94, 98, 102, 103, 104 , 105, 106, 107, 108, 112, 117 top right

Versandhaus Beate Uhse GmbH: 47, 80, 88

Victoria & Albert Museum: 56 bottom

Video Team: 11

World of Wonder: 27

World of Wonder: 53 top (Sarah Mortimer), 147, 149 middle and bottom, 150 (Fenton Bailey), 151 top sequence, 160 top, 165 bottom,

Zane Entertainment: 165 top sequence of three